**"Man, what a jerk I've been
to trust that preacher," I scoffed bitterly.**
I had allowed David Wilkerson to enter my "inner turf." I had trusted him as I had never trusted anybody else. All my life it had been hammered into my head not to trust anybody. Now I had found out the hard way. "How could I have ever believed in God, in something I can't even see? Man, I've been had!"

Suddenly my mind was made up. I dumped the contents of the duffel bag onto the bed. I picked up my Bible.

"I won't be needing this anymore. There ain't no God and this book's nothing but a bunch of lies!"

I ran to the window, swung my arm back, and threw the Bible as hard as I could against the pane. The book smashed through the glass and sailed through the air. Five stories below on St. Edward Street, it hit the pavement with a thump. It fell open and some pages, ruffling in the wind, tore free of their binding and scattered all over the street.

I had no way of knowing that the next ten years of my life were going to be scattered to the wind, just like those pages. . . .

Second Chance

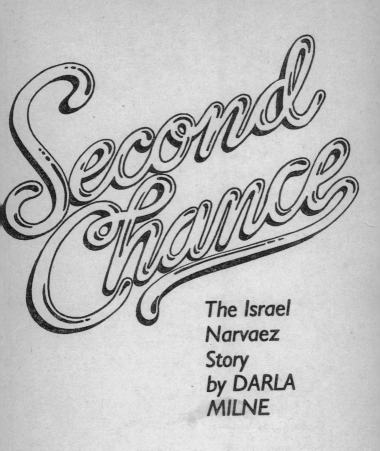

The Israel
Narvaez
Story
by DARLA
MILNE

LIVING BOOKS
Tyndale House Publishers, Inc.
Wheaton, Illinois

Library of Congress
Catalog Card Number
79-63829
ISBN, 0-8423-5843-9,
paper
Copyright © 1979 by
Israel Narvaez and
Darla Milne. All rights
reserved.
First printing,
January 1980.
Printed in the United
States of America.

CONTENTS

FOREWORD

In the few years I've known Israel Narvaez, I've seen all kinds of people, from the tender young girl to the tough, hard-bitten man, respond to his challenge to accept Christ. Challenge is the word, because Israel's testimony leaves no room for lame excuses. If God can save "Izzy," he can save anyone. But telling that story has been costly.

For instance, Israel led thirteen young boys in Canada to Christ. Less than a month later, a boat carrying those same boys overturned and all were drowned. Billy Graham mentioned the tragedy in a radio broadcast, thanking God for their conversion and salvation. But depressed by the sad tidings and exhausted from overwork (he labors full-time in a factory to support his family), Israel had an epileptic seizure while driving on the freeway. His car careened down the ditch separating the lanes. Rolling over several times, the car was so badly damaged that workmen had to cut him out with a torch. Miraculously, he survived with just a few bruises—the cost of discipleship.

He reminds me of Rocky Graziano, a fighter with a lot of heart. In fighting his spiritual battles Israel's taken some pretty good shots. However, he won't stay down; he's stubborn. Even if it kills him, Israel will never stop preaching Jesus Christ. How many of us can say the same?

Matthew 21:28 tells of a father and two sons. The first son is asked to do a work and readily agrees, but then doesn't carry through. So the father asks the second son, who stubbornly refuses, but then repents and does his father's will.

Israel is like the second son. He is stubborn but also determined. His determination has brought hundreds to a saving knowledge of our Lord. His stubbornness has lost him some friends. He is determined to fight the good fight his way, with no other authority over him than Christ himself. Consequently, he has preached in places few well-known evangelists have gone. He has been available to the little guy in the out-of-the-way church, jail, school, or hall. But it has cost him, financially and physically.

It is my prayer that after having read his story, many will come to know and respect this soldier for Christ as I have, to the glory of God. God's ministry is more than patent leather shoes and new suits; it is real people fighting the devil. I praise God for brave men like Israel who have the heart to fight for Jesus Christ.

Stephen T. Hillis
Sheldon Jackson College
Sitka, Alaska

8

ONE
The Turning Point

The headlines of the New York *Daily News* for
Tuesday, February 24, 1959, read:

BOY, 17, SLAIN IN TEEN GANG WAR

And another one, a few days later:

4 IN GANG KILLING CLOWN IN COURT
AND 4 MOTHERS WEEP

Below the headlines was printed a photograph
of four grinning youths surrounded by police.
The caption identified the one on the right as
Israel Narvaez, age sixteen. That was me. Sixteen years old and arrested for murder.

Less than seven months before, I had become a
Christian.

What happened in those few short months to
turn me—a promising young Christian, who
Rev. David Wilkerson had once believed could

become a "giant for the Lord"—into an accomplice to murder?

The turning point in my new life occurred one Saturday in the early fall of 1958. When I woke up that morning, I was not prepared for the tragic misunderstanding that was about to take place, nor for the rapid sequence of events that followed.

A faint light filtered in through the window. I pushed aside the bedcovers and, in the darkness, groped for my pants. In the next bed my younger brother David, who had suffered an asthma attack during the night, was now sleeping peacefully. As I pulled on my pants, I was careful not to disturb him. His wheezing had kept me awake for most of the night, but I hadn't minded—I had a soft spot for this seven-year-old brother of mine. Besides, I had been much too excited to sleep. All night I had tossed and turned on my bed, restlessly counting the hours to daybreak. Now that dawn had almost broken, my big adventure was about to begin.

In the bathroom, I splashed cold water on my face and sponged my neck and shoulders. I thrust my chin close to the small mirror above the sink basin, searching hopefully for the slightest whisker stubble, but as usual my skin was chalk-smooth. Disappointed—for at sixteen I was in a hurry to begin shaving—I turned my attention to my hair. Squeezing a generous dab of Dixie-Peach gel on the palm of my hand, I greased my corkscrew curls down flat against my scalp. Then, reaching in my hip pocket for my comb, I slicked the hair around my temples back with an expert flick of the wrist and patted my ducktail into place in late-1950s style. As the final touch, I twisted my long greasy bangs, which drooped down over my eyebrows, into a neat Tony Curtis curl.

Satisfied, I stepped back to examine my reflection. All my features, the thick mass of wavy black hair, the coal-black eyes, the sallow Puerto Rican complexion, the solid row of even white teeth, were the same as ever—only my expression had changed in the last few months. Once it had been mean, hard, and hostile; it was now open, relaxed, and even friendly. The "no-trespassing sign" I had worn had been replaced with a "welcome mat."

"Man, Israel baby," I grinned, making a cocky thumbs-up sign to my mirror image. "You are one handsome dude."

As I walked back into my bedroom, I buttoned my shirt and tucked the tail neatly into my slacks. David was still sleeping, so I tiptoed over to the corner of the room where the duffel bag I had borrowed from my brother Manny was propped up against the wall. Last night as I had been packing, David had sat on his bed cross-legged, chin on his fist, watching me curiously.

"Watcha doin', Israel?" he had asked me.

"Packin'." I had stated the obvious.

"How come?"

"Cause I'm goin' on a trip . . ."

"Yeah?" His shoe-button eyes had opened wide. "Where you goin'? Past the Brooklyn Bridge?"

" 'Way past the Brooklyn Bridge, man," I had grinned. "Right out of New York State."

"Wow!"

"I'm goin' to the country," I boasted proudly. That may not be a big deal to most people, but to me—a boy from the Brooklyn ghetto who had only been out of New York City twice since I had emigrated from Puerto Rico at age three—it was an exciting event. One of the highlights of my life.

"Will you see cows and horses and everything . . . ?" David had asked me eagerly.

"Yup," I nodded. "And chickens and pigs [David wrinkled his nose] and apple trees and farms." I was especially interested in seeing those cows. I loved chocolate milk and had heard that it came from brown cows. Now I was going to get a chance to check them out. Of course, I didn't know how to get the milk out of the cow, but I figured that someone would teach me. Then I would be able to guzzle down all the chocolate milk I wanted.

"Can I come too, Israel?" David had pleaded with me.

"Nah. You ain't old enough yet. Besides, the preacher didn't invite you. He only invited me and Nicky."

Rev. David Wilkerson had invited us to his country church in the town of Philipsburg, Pennsylvania, to meet the people who had been praying for us. He had told us so much about these good farmers, who had sacrificed greatly to send him back and forth to minister in the ghettos of New York, that I was really looking forward to meeting them. I had no idea where Philipsburg was, but I knew that it was in the country and that's all that mattered. When I thought of the country, I pictured miles and miles of flat, wide, open land—the plains I had seen in so many cowboy movies. Of course, I had no way of knowing that Pennsylvania was mountainous.

I had stuffed everything into the duffel bag that I would be needing in the next few days. I wasn't taking much with me: a pair of dungarees, a knit shirt, a few toiletry items, and my big Bible. The Bible took up the most space and weighed three times as much as anything else, but I didn't mind. It had recently become my most treasured possession.

Now I swung the duffel bag up over my shoulder and stuffed the dollar bills, which my mother had left for me on the dresser, into my pocket. As I grabbed my good jacket off its hanger in the closet—the one that I always wore on special occasions like mass or school assemblies—I could almost hear my mother saying:

"I don't want no son of mine looking like a bum."

I closed the door softly and walked down the hall to the kitchen, passing the other three bedrooms where the rest of my family was still sleeping soundly. There were eleven of us all together, but my father, a merchant marine, was away at sea again on one of his extended voyages. My oldest sister Aurelia had married and moved into her own place; and as for my oldest brother Benjamin—he came and went at odd hours of the day and night. Nobody could keep track of him.

In the kitchen I boiled some water on the stove and made myself a cup of coffee. I gulped it down, not bothering to sit at the table. Through the window, I could see the pink streaks of dawn lightening the sky; I was anxious to be off. I slung the duffel bag over my shoulder once again and closed the apartment door behind me. I didn't wait to take the elevator but bounded down the flight of stairs to ground level.

Outside it was light already. The rising sun, reflected in each of the thousands of windows of the towering Ft. Greene Housing Project apartment buildings, caused the dirty glass, brick, and concrete to glow like fire. The rays weren't strong enough yet to dispel the thin early morning fog, nor to evaporate the pools of water along the gutter. Overhead, the widening patches of blue sky indicated that it was going to be a beautiful day.

Even at this hour of the morning the streets weren't deserted. Taxicabs ran back and forth. As I strolled down St. Edward Street, I passed a few hobos—ragged men who were not as old as they looked—and an alley cat scrounging for its breakfast in an overturned garbage can. I passed P.S. 67, the school which I had attended irregularly until grade eight, the Walt Whitman Library, and the large Catholic church, Michael-St. Edwards, where my mother had occasionally dragged me to mass.

As I reached Auburn Street, I came to the corner where I had first heard Rev. Wilkerson preaching. I had been president of the MauMaus then. Could it only have been a few months ago? I remembered that lazy summer midafternoon when I had first met Rev. Wilkerson, as if it had been yesterday. . . .

I and fifteen other members of my gang, the MauMaus, had been lounging in the park in the heart of the Ft. Greene Project, our usual hangout. We had been sprawled out on the grass, smoking cigarettes and marijuana, tipping back half-gallon jugs of Thunderbird and Muscatel, cheap wines. Our transistor radios had blasted out the latest tunes, mostly rhythm 'n blues mingled with rock 'n roll. When Bill Haley and the Comets' new hit "Rock Around the Clock" had been announced, I had sprung to my feet.

"Hey c'mon, man," I urged three of the others to join me. "Let's sing along."

"Yeah, baby. This is my favorite!"

Entertaining the other MauMaus, we crooned along with the Comets, snapping our fingers to the catchy beat:

"One o'clock, two o'clock, three o'clock rock. . . ."

As the song ended, the blaring of a distant trumpet competed with our radios.

"Hey, man, what's happening?" Nicky Cruz, the vice-president of our gang asked, rolling over on his stomach.

"Sounds like a circus or something," Paco offered.

"Cool. Let's bebop over right now and find

out," I suggested. If the trumpet was announcing the arrival of a circus, the MauMaus wanted to be in on the action. A circus meant people with their pockets full of cash. Besides, we were bored and a circus would create a welcome diversion: rides, balloons, games, and prizes. I stooped over to pick up my black leather jacket and alpine hat—which I carried, not wanting to mess my neatly slicked-down hair—and put on my sunglasses. As I climbed up the grassy slope, the others followed.

Dominating the sidewalk, we jitter-bugged down St. Edward Street, bobbing and weaving like the swelling waves of the Atlantic Ocean. Two blocks ahead of us, near the corner of Auburn Street, we could see a growing group of curiosity seekers milling around a trumpet player. The player himself was obscured from our vision by a lamp post, but the polished brass of his trumpet gleamed golden in the sunlight. Housewives, intrigued by the lively tune, poked their heads out of the project apartment windows above, while children danced on the street, darting in and out of the crowd.

"Hey, man, ain't that the dude whose picture was in all the papers?" Sardine nudged me, as we hovered on the edge of the crowd. He pointed to a thin man standing quietly beside the trumpet player, head slightly bowed. The man had high cheekbones, buck teeth, and blond cornsilk hair. He was so skinny that I thought he looked like a scarecrow escaped from a cornfield.

"Yeah, baby, you're right," I agreed, recognizing the man's face. "He's that crazy country preacher who got kicked out of the Dragons' trial. . . ."

In the papers we had read that Rev. David Wilkerson had gone to the courtroom where the members of the Dragon gang were being tried for the cruel murder of a fifteen-year-old polio victim. Intending to speak in the boys' defense, he had instead been thrown out of court. We reasoned that if the cops were against him, he must be on our side. Getting into trouble with the law was like a credit card in the ghettos. We'd stick around and listen to what he had to say.

As soon as he opened his mouth, his accent confirmed that he wasn't from Brooklyn, or for that matter, New York. Speaking with a drawl like John Wayne, he told us that he had some good news for us.

"Man," I thought to myself cynically, "what kind of good news could he have for us?" All we ever heard was bad news. We were bad news itself.

With his slow midwestern twang he continued, "I want to talk to you folks today about a Scripture verse. It's called John 3:16."

I had to stop myself from bursting into laughter. Who ever heard of anyone being called John Three-sixteen?

"Well, dig it, man," the MauMau standing beside me wisecracked, "maybe his parents are mathematicians and they call him 316 for short."

I snickered and slapped his palm. The preacher had just opened his black book when we noticed the police coming. "Hey, here comes the heat!"

The policeman walked through the crowd up to the stranger. "What are you trying to do here, mister? Start a riot or something?"

The preacher looked surprised. "No. I'm a minister and I've come to preach the gospel to these folks."

"Well, you're not going to do any preaching around here, mister. You're starting a riot. Look at how excited these hoodlums are. Like a bunch of vultures just waiting to kill somebody. C'mon, let's go."

"Sir, don't I have the right to preach the gospel on any street corner that I want to in this country?" the minister inquired calmly. "Isn't that in the constitution?"

"That's right, buddy. But you've only got it half right. You've got to speak under an American flag. And you don't have one."

Just then a sergeant joined the police officer and asked, "What's going on here?"

"This man wants to tell these kids about the love of God."

"Well, that should be a good experience for them. They need all the love they can get," the sergeant replied. "Look, you go on with your beat. I'll keep an eye on the situation."

As the police officer started to walk away, scowling, Paco grabbed a little American flag that was flying from the radio antenna of a car parked at the curb.

"Hey, dig it man," he waved the miniature flag in front of the policeman's face. "The dude got a flag now."

"That isn't a flag!" the policeman contradicted him.

"Hey, man, what do you mean, this ain't no flag?" the MauMau cried indignantly. "This is an American flag, man. You mustn't be an American. Don't you know the color of your flag?"

"That's just a toy," he scoffed.

"Man, don't you know anything about the law? In a time of need, this little piece of cloth represents the flag of our country. And if this ain't a time of need, I dunno when the time of need is ever gonna be!" The boy had them on a legal technicality. The policeman shook his head and walked away. The sergeant grinned and told the boy to hold the flag up.

"Right on, baby. I'm a human flagpole." Everybody laughed. We all enjoyed spiting the law. We had a joke among the MauMaus: "The police enforce the law and we deforce it."

The preacher continued his speech. He told us one of the biggest fairy tales I had ever heard—and I had heard a lot, but nothing like this. He told us about some dude who had come down from his Kingdom of heaven to die for us. Because of my Catholic upbringing I had heard about Jesus, but I had never given him much thought. Even now as the preacher was speaking, I was listening more to his fascinating accent than to his words. He spoke with sincerity, but what he was saying was all just a bunch of baloney to me. And it was obvious that he believed it—even if nobody else did. I thought he was a harmless fool.

When he finished speaking, he asked us to bow our heads. Of course, we didn't. Then he asked if there was anyone who would like to invite this Jesus into his life. To my surprise, first one boy and then another and another raised their hands. They weren't members of my gang, so I didn't care, but I wondered what kind of hocus-pocus was going on. The preacher made the boys kneel down on the street. I couldn't believe that something like this was happening in broad daylight. Afterward the preacher came around to shake our hands.

"Can I shake your hand?" he asked me. He wasn't smiling, but he had a kind of weird smile in his eyes.

"Well, we don't shake hands like you do, man. We got our own way of doin' it. Give me five, man. That's right. Just hold out your hand." He held his hand out and I slapped his palm. I was friendly enough to this preacher. As a Catholic, I had been taught to respect men of the cloth, and even though this man wasn't dressed like a priest, he was one of sorts. He didn't pose a threat to me. Not so, apparently, for Nicky.

"Can I shake your hand, young man?" he asked Nicky, who was standing right beside me. Nicky glared at him, then slapped him across the face.

"Man," I snickered to myself. "Somebody's gonna get done in real bad." I was expecting to see a good fight. Maybe this skinny preacher was stronger than he looked.

But instead of swinging his fist, the preacher

said in a calm voice that held no trace of anger, "Young man, Jesus loves you."

Nicky stared at him in disbelief. He didn't know what was going on. He looked at me. I shrugged. We had never encountered anything like this before. . . .

As the preacher took a step toward Nicky, something clicked in the same instant. I knew that sound well—my life depended upon it. Nicky pointed his opened switchblade at the preacher's throat. Strangely, the sergeant, who had a .38 special, didn't attempt to interfere.

"Look, young man," the preacher said calmly, "you can take that knife and cut me up in a thousand pieces—I doubt if you'll get a thousand pieces off of me anyway—but I'm going to tell you something. Each piece is going to cry out, 'Jesus loves you. Jesus loves you.'"

"Aw, man, you're crazy," Nicky sneered. "Get out of my face." He turned and walked away.

Although I didn't buy what the preacher was selling, I admired his courage. This incident made a profound impression upon me. Baffled, I couldn't figure this skinny preacher-dude out at all.

If we thought we had seen the last of this crazy preacher, we were wrong. A few weeks later, when we were planning a big gang rumble on Coney Island (it was going to be a July-the-fourth free-for-all, but instead of popping firecrackers we were going to pop teeth and crack heads), Rev. Wilkerson approached us again. As he walked down the block toward us, I snickered because he reminded me of a skeleton left over from Halloween. This time he invited us to an inter-city youth rally he was holding at St. Nicholas Arena for all the gangs in New York City.

"Man, you're crazy! You know what's gonna happen if you get all those gangs in one place at one time?" I asked him incredulously, appalled at his ignorance.

"No," he answered innocently.

"You're gonna have World War Three on your hands!"

"No," he said, "the Spirit of the Lord hath anointed me to—."

"Yeah, I know. Jesus loves you and all that stuff. I'll catch you later, man. I know you're crazy now!" I turned to walk away.

"Israel!" he shouted after me. "Are you a chicken?"

I stopped, stunned. Being called a chicken was like getting slapped in the face twice. Nobody dared to call a MauMau a chicken. I stared at him in disbelief. He looked at me with his baby blue eyes with their Jesus look and funny smile.

"Are you going to come?" he asked me.

"Yeah," I replied angrily. "I'm gonna come, preacher. But you know why I'm gonna come? Because there's gonna be a big gang war there and I wanna be in on the action!"

"Oh, good. Wonderful," he beamed with delight. "I hope you bring all your gang with you."

As I turned to go for the second time, the preacher stopped me. "Wait a minute. I'm not done yet . . ."

"What do you want me to do now?" I asked sarcastically. "Sing hallelujah?"

"Well, that would be a beginning."

I was so astonished I could only stare at him. The man was crazy! A religious nut.

"Look," he said, "I'll arrange for a bus to pick you and your gang up Saturday evening and I'll drive you to St. Nick's so you won't get into trouble on the subways."

But when the night of the rally came, instead of leading my gang in a rumble, I led them to the altar.

As I had sat unwillingly, listening to Rev. Wilkerson preach about this Man Jesus who had personally died for me, a strange thing had happened. I wasn't easily moved by emotion, but when I pictured the lonely figure of that Man crumpled on the cross, when I thought of how much he loved me and how much he had suffered, something within me broke. The proud Empire State Building of my heart came crashing down.

Somehow, I felt the tears pricking my eyes. Embarrassed, I fiercely tried to hold them back. I wasn't about to cry. Not me! No way! The President of the MauMaus just doesn't cry—that stuff was for sissies. To my horror, a tear rolled down my cheek. Quickly I brushed it away, looking around to make sure that nobody had seen it. Then I wiped away another and another.

"Man, what's happening to me?"

When the preacher asked all those who wanted

to invite this Jesus into their lives to come to the platform, I rushed to the front. Now I didn't care who saw me. I knew that this was what I needed and wanted. Some of the members of my gang, including Nicky the vice-president—the same Nicky who had once held nothing but contempt for the preacher and his message—followed me. That night, Jesus became a reality in our lives.

After Rev. Wilkerson prayed for us, he handed out Bibles, pocket-sized editions and large black editions with gold lettering on the front.

"How come we can't have one of those bigger Bibles?" one of the MauMaus cried out. "We want the whole world to know that we're jitter-bugging for Jesus now!" Everybody grinned.

"Yeah," I added my two cents. "Lemme have one of those too." I grabbed the large edition and flipped curiously through its pages. At the top of a page, I noticed my own name, Israel. Further down the page, I saw my name written three or four more times.

"Hey, preacher, look!" I shouted. "My name's written all over the pages here. It's all over this book." He grinned back at me.

With my name mentioned so many times in the Bible, I knew for sure that God must have something special planned for my life.

Now, excited about seeing Rev. Wilkerson again, I turned onto Myrtle Avenue and covered the three blocks to Flatbush Avenue quickly. On the corner of Flatbush and Myrtle, I propped my duffel bag against the lamp post and relaxed.

I was early. In an hour—at 7:00 A.M. sharp—the Christian attorney, a friend of Rev. Wilkerson, would be coming to pick me up. He would drive me to his hometown parish in Pennsylvania. I could hardly wait.

TWO
Left Standing

> Be sober, be vigilant; because your adver-
> sary the devil, as a roaring lion, walketh
> about, seeking whom he may devour:
> Whom resist stedfast in the faith . . .
> (1 Peter 5:8, 9).

The hour passed quickly. I stood on the corner,
cheerfully whistling the tune of a song I had
recently learned: "Washed in the Blood of the
Lamb." In the weeks following the youth rally,
my buddy Nicky and I had been attending a
local Spanish church almost every night and had
learned many wonderful songs of praise and worship.

Across Flatbush Avenue, a large electric Pepsi
clock in the darkened window of a restaurant
kept me constantly aware of the exact time. At
five minutes to seven, I picked up my duffel bag
and stepped to the edge of the curb, eagerly

26

watching the approach of every car, hoping each one in turn would be the Christian attorney's car. I didn't know what kind of car he would be driving but I expected him to spot me first and pull over to the curb. We had met each other a few times before so he would have no trouble recognizing me. There was no way he could miss me. Car after car whizzed by.

I glanced at the restaurant clock impatiently: 7:15. "What's keeping those dudes?" I grumbled. I did not like to be kept waiting. I was anxious to begin the trip and leave New York City far behind. "C'mon, you guys. Hurry up. Let's get a move on. . . ." I scuffed my heel against the curb in agitation. Overhead, a train rattled by on the elevated track.

At 7:30, a plump, middle-aged man dressed in a shabby trench coat, stopped in front of the door of the restaurant across the street. He searched in his pockets for the keys, unlocked the door, and disappeared inside. A few minutes later, the lights came on and the *Closed* sign was removed from the window; the restaurant was now open for business. People began to go in and out for coffee or to grab a quick breakfast. By now I was beginning to feel hungry myself and wished I had taken the time to make myself a couple of slices of toast. If I had known the attorney was going to be this late. . . . Briefly, I toyed with the idea of running across the street and grabbing a chocolate bar—once we hit the road it might be many hours before we would stop for lunch. I gave up the idea, however, because I was taking absolutely no chances of missing my ride.

"Where are they?" I scowled, rocking on the balls of my feet in my impatience. "They should have been here ages ago!" I began to make up all sorts of excuses for their tardiness. "Maybe the attorney's alarm clock didn't go off," I suggested hopefully, "and he slept in. Or maybe Nicky wasn't ready on time. Or maybe they had a flat tire. Or . . ."

By 8:00, I knew something was wrong—desperately wrong. Exhausted from the strain of examining every passing vehicle, I slumped against the lamp post. I looked angrily in the direction that the attorney should be coming from, and then looked in the other direction at the Brooklyn Bridge, which we should have crossed a whole hour ago. "They better have a good excuse," I muttered fiercely.

The el train rumbled by overhead again. Three boys stumbled out of the covered flight of stairs leading down from the elevated train platform across Myrtle Avenue. Dazzled by the brilliant sunlight, they hesitated on the corner for a minute. From their groggy manner and rumpled clothing, I could tell that they had spent the night riding the trains. Upon closer inspection I realized that they were members of a rival gang. They looked mean and in bad humor this morning; I wanted nothing to do with them.

"Man, I hope they don't recognize me!" I growled, aware of the vulnerable position I was in. A sitting duck. Three against one were not the kind of odds I favored. From experience, I knew only too well what happened to lone "strays" like myself.

And then another thought occurred to me. "Even if they don't recognize me as a MauMau," I groaned, "the way I'm dolled up, they'll probably think I've got a lot of cash stashed on me!"

Nervously I eyed them—prepared to run if I had to. I shoved the duffel bag tightly under my left arm and slipped my hand inside the opening, hoping they would think I was trying to conceal a gun. Then, just as the threesome was about to cross Myrtle Avenue to my corner, for no reason at all, they changed their mind and crossed Flatbush Avenue instead. Across the street, they passed by the restaurant and continued down the avenue, not giving me a second glance. I heaved a sigh of relief, but the incident left me feeling uneasy. It made me want to get out of this city all the more. Fervently, I wished that the attorney's car would miraculously appear.

"They'll be here any minute now," I comforted myself, with more confidence than I really felt. "They'll be here. I know they will!"

I squeezed my duffel bag, feeling the hard edge of my Bible inside. That calmed me down somewhat. When I had first spotted those rival gang members, my first reaction had been to panic. Without a weapon, I felt helpless, almost naked. I had depended on a switchblade for protection for so many years that I found it difficult to trust now in God alone.

One of my first acts after committing my life to Christ had been to turn over all my weapons to the police. I had gathered them from under my mattress where I had stowed them for safe-keeping. I threw them into a shopping bag—machetes, brass knuckles, chains, switchblades, and zipguns—everything. Then Nicky and I and a few of the other converted MauMaus had trooped over to the local police station. Upon entering the door, however, my shopping bag's bottom had ripped apart and all my assorted artillery had clattered to the floor in front of the policemen on duty. Automatically, I had thrown my hands up in surrender—in case they thought we had been about to attack.

Quickly we had explained to the astonished police our purpose for coming. We had told them that we had no need for weapons anymore: we were through with fighting and killing, we were now going to serve Jesus. The police, amazed and unbelieving, had had to phone Rev. Wilkerson to verify our incredible story. Now, in exchange for the "hardware," I had a Bible with all the policemen's autographs on the inside flap.

Lately, that Bible had become very precious to me. Every day since the youth rally, I had pored over its pages, concentrating mainly on the Old Testament stories. Some of them were already familiar to me because I had seen them drama-tized at the movies. My favorite ones were about Samson and Delilah, David and Goliath, Moses, Abraham, Jacob, and Joseph. I was especially interested in Samson's story—how he had turned his back on God and consequently lost his strength, his eyesight, and finally his life. I was also impressed with the story of Joseph and how he had been "sold out" by his own family, the people he had loved the most. (Perhaps, in view of what was about to happen to me, God was using these stories to speak to me.) Of course, being only a newly born Christian, I hadn't understood much of what I had read. I had really only started to study God's Word and learn what he had to say to me.

Now, as I waited on the street corner, I paced back and forth on the sidewalk. The Saturday morning traffic on Flatbush Avenue's eight lanes had picked up considerably. The city was roaring to life. In the distance, the three boys disappeared down a side street.

My close call with them made me remember all the times in recent weeks that I had brushed with my former fellow gang members. Although I had tried to stay away from former hangouts, I found it impossible to avoid them entirely. Often, on my way to the grocery store, I would pass a few MauMaus loitering on the street corner. They would snicker and insult me.

"Here comes the Hallelujah Boy," one would jeer.

"Hey, saint. Your halo's slipping," another taunted.

I hated being the object of ridicule. It was a new experience for me. Once I had commanded these very same boys' respect and esteem; now I had only their scorn. I felt bitter. Nobody likes to fall from the top rung of the ladder to the bottom of the barrel.

The constant name-calling and needling was beginning to wear me down. Sometimes I had the almost overpowering urge to smash the hecklers in the face, but I wrestled with this impulse. I knew it was wrong. That was the old Israel trying to take control—but I was a brand new person in Christ.

The MauMaus believed that anyone who "got religion" was a square, and worse, a coward. Although they were still wary of my former reputation as a fighter, they mocked me and dared me to fight back. Knowing that I could beat them, knowing they were afraid of me—that was the worst part. All I could do was try to ignore them. But I was tired of being hassled.

People brushed by me on their way to the subway station. I watched them sadly. Everyone seemed to be going somewhere—everyone but me. I felt foolish just standing there and I was getting tired. I wanted to sit down on the curb, but I didn't want to dirty my good pants. I shifted the duffel bag from under one arm to the other and finally propped it up against the street lamp again. The el train rumbled by every half hour. 9:00. 9:30. 10:00 . . .

"Where are they? Where are they?" I cried in frustration. "They've got to come! They've got to." I wouldn't give up hope yet.

"Maybe you should just go home," the thought pricked my pride. "You've been stood up. . . ."

"No," I resisted firmly. The preacher had promised me that the attorney would pick me up. I trusted that preacher. Men of the cloth don't lie.

By now the sun had risen high in the sky. I was getting more angry, impatient, and uncomfortable as the minutes ticked by. I tore off my jacket, threw it over my shoulder, rolled up my shirt sleeves, and undid the top three buttons of my collar. With heavy footsteps I paced back and forth, noticing that my shadow was getting shorter and shorter. Nagging doubts were picking at my mind. Something told me that I wasn't going to get out of New York after all.

As I paced the sidewalk in a bad temper, all the doubts that had besieged me in the last few months rushed to the forefront of my mind. Vividly, I recalled the night that Nicky and I, on our way to an evening service, had been shot at from a speeding car. We had instantly hit the pavement, covering our heads with our Bibles. When it was safe, we had leaped to our feet and raced to the shelter of the church. Once inside I had felt safe. My fear slipped away as I prayed and sang and concentrated on the sermon. But outside the church, it was a different story. I feared for my life. Without my gang to support me, I felt alone. Pastor Arce had told Nicky and me that the Lord was "able" and that "he would protect us," but I wasn't a hundred percent convinced. I didn't understand God's power and I wasn't sure that I was willing to risk my life for Jesus or anybody else! Already, I was wavering in my newfound faith.

Then one night Nicky had been attacked by a member of an enemy gang. Instead of fighting back, he had warded off the assailant's knife with his bare hand. He had made his way over to my apartment, his injured hand wrapped up in his T-shirt, which was soaked in blood. I had taken him to the local hospital for stitches. As we were waiting in the reception room, I had had my arms around Nicky, holding him up. He had looked so pale I had been frightened that he would pass out at any moment. I had been anxious for a doctor to see him, but critical cases kept coming in, all needing emergency treatment. (The hospital had been aptly nicknamed "the butcher shop.") It had seemed that every time they were getting ready for Nicky, another emergency case was rushed through.

As I had waited there, worrying about Nicky, I had been very uptight.

"God doesn't care about us," I had thought to myself gloomily, "or he wouldn't have let this happen to Nicky. . . ." Where was God's power now? Where was his protection?

I had been ready to go back to the gang right then and there. As I had looked at Nicky's blood-soaked, bandaged hand, I had figured that I would be the next target.

"C'mon, let's go back to the gang," I had urged Nicky. "These dudes are going to kill us! This Jesus business is for suckers." At least there was protection in the gang; safety in numbers. And besides, I was tired of being pushed. I wanted to be the one doing the pushing. I wasn't prepared to count the cost of following Christ—I wasn't prepared to be a martyr.

"No," Nicky had told me. "Let's keep on living for Jesus, man. We can make it. I know we can!"

I had been surprised by the dramatic change that had taken place in Nicky. I had thought that after what had happened to him, he would have been the first to give up and go back to the gang. Instead, he had told me that when the gang member had been stabbing him, God had given him strength and he had broken away. God *had* protected him! Then he had convinced me to give this "Jesus-stuff" another chance. Already wavering in my conviction, I had decided to wait a little longer and test it out.

When the sun was almost directly overhead, I gathered my duffel bag and jacket and walked back down Myrtle Avenue on the route I had come. It was almost noon. I was hot, hungry, and tired. I had waited five hours for the Christian attorney and that was enough; I was fed up.

"What a chump I've been," I mocked myself. I felt tricked. Conned. "All Christians are a bunch of fakes. Liars." I cursed the preacher with every dirty swear word I knew.

"This is where I get off, preacher-man. This is the last straw! I never want to see your face again."

Deeply disappointed, I blindly made my way home. I had been really counting on this trip. To me, it had come to mean much more than just a trip to the country—it was a whole new chance at life. Somehow, I thought I wouldn't just be leaving New York City behind, but my whole past. The gangs. The rumbles. The concrete prison of my existence.

Tears pricked the corners of my eyes, but I was too stubborn and bitter to cry. I had been a fool to think I could run away from Brooklyn. Who leaves the ghetto? Man, this was my turf. Where I belonged. I must have been dreaming. I was coming down from the high I had been on for the last few months. I knew it couldn't last.

"Nothing ever works out for me. . . ." I kicked a beer bottle into the gutter.

I passed the street corner where I had first heard Rev. Wilkerson preaching about the love of God. It had seemed like a silly fairy tale then; now it seemed like a cruel lie. If there was a God, he was a thousand miles away. What did he care about the hopes and plans of one insignificant Puerto Rican named Israel Narvaez? Nothing! That's what.

I climbed the stairs to the fifth floor slowly. The stale smells of urine and wine assailed my nostrils. I stepped over the broken glass, wine bottles, soiled newspapers, and garbage. When I opened the door to my apartment, my mother came out of the kitchen, hair tied in a kerchief, broom in hand.

"Israel! What are you doing back?" She looked confused. "I thought you were going to the country. . . . What happened?"

"Nah," I muttered, without meeting her eyes. "Forget it. Just forget the whole thing!"

"I told you! I told you that you shouldn't listen to those Protestants . . ." she called after me as I stormed down the hall to my room. "But you wouldn't listen to your own mother. . . ."

I shrugged and closed the bedroom door before she could say anything more. I tossed my duffel bag onto the floor and flung myself, face-down, onto my bed. My brother David had gone out to play a few hours ago. I was alone with my chaotic thoughts. After awhile, I heard my mother go out to do her shopping. I turned over on my back and stared at the ceiling.

"Man, what a jerk I've been to trust that preacher," I scoffed bitterly. I had allowed that preacher to enter my "inner turf." I had trusted him as I had never trusted anybody else. All my life it had been hammered into my head not to trust anybody. Now I had found out the hard way. "How could I have ever believed in God, in something I can't even see? Man, I've been had. These Christians are a bunch of phonies!"

Suddenly my mind was made up. I dumped the contents of the duffel bag onto the bed. I picked up my Bible.

"I won't be needing this anymore. There ain't no God and this book's nothing but a bunch of lies!"

I ran to the window, swung my arm back, and threw the Bible as hard as I could against the pane. The book smashed through the glass and sailed through the air. Five stories below on St. Edward Street, it hit the pavement with a thump. It fell open and some pages, ruffling in the wind, tore free of their binding and scattered all over the street.

I had no way of knowing that the next ten years of my life were going to be scattered to the wind, just like those pages. . . .

Take heed, brethren, lest there be in any of you an evil heart of unbelief, in departing from the living God (Heb. 3:12).

THREE
Return to the MauMaus

I turned away from the window, my faith in a
God who cares as shattered as the fragments of
glass that lay at my feet. Angrily, I strode across
the room to the closet, ripped off my good clothes,
and struggled into my old dungarees and black
leather jacket. I grabbed my alpine hat from
the top shelf, where only a few weeks ago I had
tossed it up out of sight, never expecting to wear
it again. Now I pulled it low over my brow to
shade my burning eyes, and then stormed out of
the apartment, banging the door shut behind me.

Then I made a grave mistake: I decided to
return to the gang. By changing into my old
MauMau uniform, I had already consciously
acted upon this decision.

All afternoon I stumbled blindly around the
streets. I kept my eyes on the pavement, not
caring where I was going, and almost collided

with an old woman carrying two bags of groceries. A garbage can wobbled back and forth on the sidewalk in front of me and I kicked it into the gutter. All kinds of incoherent thoughts raced through my head, along with a steady current of curse words. I wanted to cry out, but who was there to listen? I wanted to strike out in revenge, but who was there to hit? The hurt and pain inside me would not go away. I wanted to run and run until I dropped to the ground in exhaustion; I wanted to get drunk.

After five o'clock, I headed for the park in the heart of the Ft. Greene Projects. MauMau turf. By now the gang members would have started to congregate for the evening's activities. I entered the park, mounting the column of steps to the war monument on top. The park was very hilly. Underneath the mountain was an old dungeon and beside it was the crumbling castle of Ft. Greene, used now as a city jail. As I came over the hill, I could see twenty MauMaus sprawled out on the grass below, having a good time. They were in the usual hangout beside the playground, where mothers watched their children on the swings, monkey bars, and teeter-totters. Some of the MauMaus were seated on the bench on the outside of the wrought-iron fence surrounding the playground.

I approached them with confidence. After all, only a few short months ago, I had been their respected leader and now I was returning. Four or five yards away from them, I stopped. They all turned to look at me. I knew most of the guys, but a few new ones had joined the gang in my absence.

"Hey, guys, I'm back," I said simply. I didn't offer any explanations for my desertion and they asked for none. I waited for their response.

"OK, man."

"Cool."

"All right."

Most of the boys accepted me back into the gang without question. A few, however, were openly suspicious.

"Hey, what's the holy roller doing around here?" Tarzan scowled.

"Aw, shut up," I snarled. "I ain't no holy roller. I'm through with that crap."

"Man, we knew you wasn't going to hang around with those religious squares for long." Mel grinned. "You ain't the type."

"Yeah, we knew you'd be back. Sooner or later they all come back," Maximo agreed.

After that brief exchange, they showed no more curiosity. As a rule, gang members mind their own business; they leave everyone's private life private. As far as they knew, I had got religion and turned into a square. Now I had come back to my senses and was cool again. It was as simple as that. Most of the group was glad to see me back, but as I scanned their faces, I could tell that a few weren't happy about it. Especially their new leader. I threatened his position. For the moment, however, I was content just to be back among old friends. I would deal with him later . . .

I sat down on the grass and Tarzan passed me his bottle of wine, a peace-offering. I took it only too willingly, and greedily gulped it down. I wanted to blot out my thoughts and feelings, to forget this day and everything that had happened to me recently. I wanted to wipe the preacher's face and his God from my memory. I took a few tokes on a joint of marijuana that was passed to me and passed it on to the guy beside me. Two of the boys got up with their girls and stumbled off into the bushes.

I lay back on the grass and gazed blankly at the dark blue sky above. The stuff was beginning to work its magic. Already memories of the morning were fading and I was conscious only of the sweet present.

"Everything's cool," I thought. I didn't go home that evening, but instead spent the night sleeping in the park.

When my family had emigrated from Puerto Rico to New York City in 1945, we had moved into the basement of my grandparents' two-story house in the Bronx. A few years later, however, the city authorities had decided to tear down our neighborhood and we had been relocated in the low-income government housing project of Ft. Greene. Here thirty thousand people, mainly Negro and Puerto Rican, were crowded into the towering apartment buildings. Juvenile gangs had roamed the streets, protecting their turf and fighting invading gangs—stabbing, beating, and killing.

It had been here in the concrete jungle of Ft. Greene, at the age of twelve, that I had had my first confrontation with these gangs.

"Hey, man, you got any money?" a Negro youth had blocked my path one day as I had been on my way to my eighth grade class.

"Well, uh . . . yes," I had answered, surprised and confused. "I've got a couple of dimes. . . ."

"Hand them over, jack."

"Why should I give you my lunch money?" I asked indignantly.

"'Cause I want it. Dig it, man?"

"Why should I give you my lunch money?" I repeated stupidly. "If I give it to you, I'm gonna get awful hungry." I tried to get by him.

"Listen, man. *If* you don't give it to me, you ain't never gonna get hungry again!" To emphasize his point, he whipped out a knife.

When I found myself staring at the fine edge of the blade a few inches away from my throat, the twenty cents in my pocket suddenly lost their importance. "Here, take them." I thrust the change into his open palm.

Forgetting all about school, I ran home and told my mother what had happened. She didn't know what to do. In dismay, I turned to my oldest brother, Benjamin.

"C'mon. Help me beat this guy up," I pleaded.

"No way, man!"

I stared at him dumbfounded.

"Look, Israel," he explained to me patiently, "in this world you're gonna have to learn how to look out for yourself. I'm not going down there to get myself killed on account of you or anybody else. It's your battle, not mine. You've got to fight for yourself, man, because nobody else is going to."

"But you're my brother!" I cried desperately.

"Uh-uh," he shook his head. "We were brothers. This is the separating point. You're on your own now. C'mon into my room. I'm going to turn you on."

"I don't need any dope," I spluttered in exasperation. "I need something to fight that guy with."

"C'mon, just follow me."

Benjamin shut the door behind me and then walked over to the bunkbed. When he lifted the mattress, I gasped in astonishment at the collection of knives, chains, brass knuckles, and other weapons he had hidden there.

"Here." He dropped a pearl handle into my hand.

"What am I going to do with a stupid broken knife handle?" I snorted. "If I go take one of Mom's kitchen knives I've got a better chance."

"Boy, you sure are a square, aren't you?" my brother said scornfully. "That's a switchblade. It's got a concealed blade. Look, I'll show you how it works." He pointed out the safety catch button and the button that opened the blade. I pressed it.

"Aiee . . ." I stifled a scream, finding myself holding the sharp blade in my hand while the handle was up in the air. I had almost cut my fingers off. "This thing's dangerous."

"That's the idea," my brother quipped.

I practiced opening the switchblade. "Wow, this is neat."

The following day, the same Negro boy was waiting for me at school again.

"OK, jack, hand it over. He was confident that because he had taken the money so easily the first time, the second time was going to be even easier. But he had another thing coming. Gingerly I reached into my pocket—not for the money as he thought—but for my switchblade. I pointed it at him. He stared at me, slack-jawed, not knowing what to do. I had caught him off guard. Then he made a serious mistake: he started to back up. My heart was pumping furiously, for I knew that if he pulled out his knife, I would run home again. But he didn't.

"I'm gonna get you after school," he threatened instead. "I'm a Chaplain." That didn't frighten me—I didn't know who the Chaplains were, but I was about to be introduced.

When the 3:00 bell rang, I walked out of the door into the school yard. The Negro boy was waiting for me. Only this time he had eight other Chaplains with him, all wearing leather jackets with forty-eight zippers down the front and on the sleeves. They circled me.

"So you're the dude who pulled a knife on one of my boys," a tall boy, obviously the leader, sneered. I thought he was doped up by the slow way he talked, but I later found out that this was just the gangster style.

"We're gonna blow you away, man," he drawled. I didn't understand his slang, but I didn't like the sound of it. Nor did I like the gun he had stashed in his belt—a homemade zipgun.

What am I gonna do? I panicked. *These guys mean business. They'll kill me for sure. . . .* I looked around frantically searching for an escape route, but there was none.

"Hey, what's going on here, man?" a Spanish voice behind me demanded. I whirled around. Another Puerto Rican boy stood there, leaning insolently on a bamboo cane. He wore an alpine hat with matchsticks and earrings dangling from the narrow brim, and a medallion around his neck. He was two feet shorter than I.

"This dude pulled a knife on my boy Young Blood here," the Chaplain leader replied, "and we're gonna do him in. . . ."

The Puerto Rican boy sized me up. He was the same nationality as I was.

"No way, man. That's one of my boys," he drawled, without taking his eyes off of me. "If you mess with him, man, you're gonna have to take me on."

I was surprised at his bravery. But I was even more surprised when the nine Negroes backed away.

"Hey, man, we're sorry. We didn't know he was one of your boys." The Chaplain turned to me: "Why didn't you tell us?"

"You didn't give me a chance," I bluffed.

When they walked away, my rescuer asked me, "Hey what's your name, man?"

"Israel." I sighed. My T-shirt was soaked with perspiration.

"Yeah. Dig it, man. My name's Little John the Bop. I'm president of the Apaches." He invited me to come to the park at 7:00 that night to meet the whole gang.

I agreed to come, but I wondered what I would tell my parents. That night after supper, I approached my mother.

"Mom, I'm going out to buy some book covers," I lied. "I need them for school tomorrow and . . ."

"OK," my mother consented, "but be careful. There's a lot of gangs out there and you might get yourself hurt. Come straight home." If she only knew the truth!

I entered the park, climbing the steps of the war monument on top of the hill. The park was in complete darkness. The gang had blown out the lights of the lamp posts in the surrounding area so nobody would snoop around on their turf. Even the police wouldn't dare to enter the park at night unless they were in a group of at least four.

Suddenly a dark figure stepped out of the shadows. "Hey, who are you?" he growled.

"Who, me? I'm nobody," I stammered. "My name's Israel."

"Yeah, well, what you want here?" the voice demanded.

"I'm looking for Little John the Bop," I answered nervously.

Two more youths stepped out of the shadows and asked, "What you lookin' for him for?"

"He told me to meet him here. I'm going to become a member of his gang . . . the Apaches."

"Oh, yeah? Can you prove it?"

"No, he just told me to meet him here." I shrugged helplessly.

"Well . . ." the first guy sized me up, "you don't look like you're a jitter-bug, anyway." I didn't know it at the time, but it was a gang practice to screen every unknown visitor approaching their turf, in case he was a rival gang member intent upon killing their leader.

"Little John's at the back of the monument up there with his old lady," the first shadow instructed me. I wondered what in the world his mother was doing in the park at this time of night. "Just go up there and call him . . . don't disturb him—just call his name and he'll come out."

The three shadowed youths let me pass. I mounted the steps to the top platform and circled the monument. Obeying their orders, I called out, "Are you there, Little John?"

"Yeah, man, I'm over here," a muffled voice answered from behind some bushes. "Hold on. I'll be right out."

After some rustling, he came forward to meet me. Behind him trailed a fourteen-year-old girl. He introduced me to her and to the other members of the gang. Everyone was getting ready for a rumble with the Viceroys.

"C'mon along," Little John invited me. I didn't have much choice.

"Hey, maybe I'm in luck," I thought to myself, when I noticed that all of the weapons were being passed over to the girls. "Maybe it's the girls' turn tonight to fight and all the boys have to do is watch." But then someone explained that the girls could carry the weapons in places where the police couldn't look.

A few blocks before enemy turf we met up with the girls. The weapons were distributed. I looked at the jagged pipe Little John handed to me and gulped. "What am I getting into?"

"OK, guys, let's go!" Little John waved us all forward.

Our approach had been spotted by the other gang. Suddenly it seemed like New York City was falling down. A barrage of Coke bottles, milk bottles, garbage cans, and bricks were thrown out of the apartment windows above us. Bedlam broke loose. The Viceroys charged at us, waving baseball bats and machetes.

"Man, I'm too young to die," I cried, running into the nearest building. I crouched behind a stairwell, trembling, while outside the battle raged. Then I heard a siren, and a few minutes later I could see red lights flashing. Neighbors had alerted the police and now they were rounding up the gangs and packing them into paddy wagons.

A half an hour later, when everything had settled down, I crept out of my hiding place. Then, running as fast as my sneakers could go, I cut through the alley and jumped over a fence. On the other side, I tripped over a hedge, falling on something hard. I had almost cracked my head open on a gravestone! I was in a cemetery. I peered around nervously in the darkness. I had seen a lot of horror movies, and now I found myself wondering if the ghosts of these dead people would rise up because I was stepping on their graves. Cowering behind a hedge, I decided that I was more afraid of the police than of ghosts. I waited another half hour, and then, deciding that the coast was clear, I made my way back to the fence.

Suddenly, in front of me, a shadow removed itself from behind another hedge.

"Oh-oh! One of those dead guys done rose from his grave!" Terrified, I took off in the other direction.

"Hey, wait for me!" a high-pitched voice cried behind me.

"Man, these dead guys can talk, too!" I shuddered, running even faster.

"Wait, you're going the wrong way, man. You're going back to their turf and you're gonna get hurt. C'mon, follow me. I'm an Apache."

I stopped in my tracks and turned around to face the voice. All I could see were his teeth. He grinned.

"C'mon, follow me. You're going the wrong way. C'mon, man." When I saw the bandana he had tied around his head, I knew that he was an Apache. He led me through the cemetery, back to the park.

"Hey, man, you're all right." One of the Apaches came forward and slapped my palm. There were only eight boys gathered in the park; the others had been hurt or arrested. "I saw you crack that guy's head wide open. You messed him up good."

He had mistaken me for somebody else, but knowing that gangs often murdered any members that showed cowardice, I played along with him.

"Aw, yeah, man," I boasted, "there's nothing to it."

The others readily accepted me as one of their own.

A few days later, I went to another rumble with the Apaches. This time, when the enemy gang saw us coming, they fled in the other direction.

"Hey, this ain't too bad," I thought to myself.

A week later I tagged along with four Apaches as they roamed the streets, "bebopping"—out looking for trouble. Near the candy store, we spotted a "stray"—a member of the Golden Aces, all by himself, licking an ice cream cone.

"Hey, let's have some fun. . . ." Little John the Bop smiled wickedly.

When the Golden Ace saw us, it was too late. We fell into step beside him, then shoved him into an alley.

"What you doin' around here, man? This is Apache turf." Little John slapped him around. The boy struggled, but two Apaches had him pinned firmly against the brick wall.

"Yeah, baby. We don't like Aces eating our ice cream." Vampire had taken the cone from the helpless boy and smashed it against the wall. "We're gonna teach you a lesson you'll never forget!" He fingered his switchblade, then flicked off the boy's shirt buttons one by one. He pressed the blade against the boy's throat.

"Hey, let Israel do this guy in." Little John had the bright idea.

"Cool," Vampire agreed.

Little John handed me his knife. "Cut his gut wide open, man."

I stared at the knife blade and then I looked up at the frightened Ace's face. I had nothing against the boy. I had never seen him before. Why should I kill him?

"C'mon, man," Little John said impatiently, "go ahead."

I clenched the knife and turned my head away. I closed my eyes. Then I jabbed the knife blindly at the boy.

"Ahhh . . ." the boy gurgled and I knew I had hit him. I turned around to see the ashen-faced youth slump to the pavement. The two Apaches let him fall.

I bent over the body and tried to pull the knife out. It was stuck and didn't come out very easily. I jerked it out and as I did so, I heard a queer hissing sound escaping from the boy's punctured lungs. I thought I was going to be sick.

"Hey, man, you done a good job." The others patted me on the back. "*We'll* finish him off. . . ." They kicked his body with their pointed shoes. Little John then ground his heel into the Ace's face.

"C'mon, let's split," Little John ordered us, and we all ran down the back alley.

"I did it! I did it!" I shouted to myself as I ran. I shivered from the thrill it gave me. The sickening sensation had been replaced with a heady wild joy. "Now I'm really an Apache!"

After that, I started to look forward to rumbles and the chance to knife somebody. The more I did it—the better I got at it. It became easy, as easy as cutting a cake, and a whole lot more fun.

In the park, the Apaches lounged on the grass, boasting about their exploits, drinking and getting high. The boys passed around jugs of cheap wine. They passed the bottle to me. Wanting to be "cool," I took a big gulp. I felt a soothing, warm sensation in my stomach.

"Hey, there's nothing to this," I thought smugly. I took another slug, and then another.

"Hold on there," another boy laughed. "Save some for us. If you drink too much of that stuff, you're gonna get drunk."

"Nah," I shrugged, "this stuff is just like fruit juice." But already I felt lightheaded. I decided I enjoyed the feeling. The other gang members alternated the wine with marijuana.

"Hey, man, take a toke. You gotta try this." They were always after me to try pot.

"Nah." I'd push the marijuana joint away, remembering how I had choked on my first tobacco cigarette.

They would look at me as if I was square. "You don't know what you're missing, man. This stuff is good. It's dynamite. It'll blow you up."

"Nah, later, man," I would always say. "I'm not interested in that stuff."

But it wasn't long before I succumbed to their pressure. When the others tired of marijuana, seeking a bigger thrill, they started to skin-pop heroin—not injecting it into their veins, but just under the surface of the skin with a needle. Others sniffed it through their noses. I hated the sight of needles and one of the Apaches warned me, "If you sniff that stuff, man, you're gonna burn out your nostrils."

That didn't appeal to me. "Yeah," I told him, "that stuff ain't for me. I wanna keep breathing."

Most of the Apaches began to get more interested in getting high than in rumbling. The other Apaches spent an increasing amount of time stealing to support their ever-growing habit. "When you get the monkey on your back, you've got to feed it." A lot of the other boys began to drop out of the gang gradually to support their habit full time. Or they were arrested by the police for burglary. The Apache gang began to disintegrate.

One day I decided I had to make my break with the gang. I was tired of sitting around getting high. Fighting gave me my real kicks.

"I'm gonna join another gang—one that fights," I told Little John the Bop. I had been with the Apaches for over a year. "I'll catch you guys later. . . ."

"Hey, man," Little John tried to stop me, "if you do that, someday you're gonna have to fight against me."

I looked at him sadly. "Well, the way things look right now, there won't be much of a fight, will there?" I turned to walk away. They let me go. I had built a solid reputation as a nasty customer by now and nobody wanted to take me on.

"Wait, man, we're coming with you." Five other Apaches who liked to rumble followed me.

As we walked through the park, discussing

which gang we should join, one of the others suggested, "Hey, why don't we form our own gang?"

We liked the idea. "Cool. I can dig that."

"Yeah, baby. Crazy." All six of us agreed.

"What should we call ourselves?"

"How about the MauMaus—after that African tribe?" one of the six suggested. All of us had read about the fearful blood-thirsty tribe raiding across Africa killing missionaries.

"Yeah, that's it—the MauMaus—Murder Incorporated." We slapped each other's palms.

"Now we need a leader." I turned to the two oldest boys. They were sixteen years old, tall and muscular.

"Uh-uh. Not me," they both backed away.

"How about you, Israel?" the others addressed me. I was thirteen, going on fourteen.

"No way," I shook my head vehemently, "I don't want to be no leader."

"C'mon. Why not?" they urged.

"Uh-uh. Too much responsibility." I turned them down. The leader had to be the thinker. He planned all the attack strategies. He had to take the first step and be the most daring, the most courageous. He had to face the challenges from the others and handle the rebels. And he had to keep his distance from the others, remain aloof. Be a loner.

"Aw, go on, man. You be the leader, OK?"

"Well," I shrugged, finally relenting. "If that's what you guys want. . . ." Actually, the position of leader carried its own fringe benefits. First choice of the girls, for example.

"Cool, baby. You're our new leader." They slapped my palm.

Under my leadership, the MauMaus soon earned the reputation of one of the toughest, most feared gangs in Brooklyn. Our name had become synonymous with terror.

Now, after turning my back on God, I had returned to this life of violence and hatred. I had rejected Christianity and rejoined the MauMaus.

One evening at the end of my first week back with the gang, I decided to confront the new leader. After all, why should I be satisfied with a back-seat position when I could be the number-one dude?

I got to my feet. "I wanna be your president again," I declared boldly, daring anyone to challenge me. I watched the MauMaus' faces closely for any hint of rebellion. A few of the guys just kept on dancing to the radio music with their debs. The others waited to see what would happen next.

"Oh, yeah?" Panamania got to his feet, swaying a little. He was a dark-skinned, frizzy-haired fifteen-year-old from Panama. He was new to the gang and had assumed the role of president after I had defected. He didn't like the idea of losing his position so soon, but he wasn't sure what he could do about it. I took advantage of his uncertainty.

"That's right. Any objections?" I gave him a cold, hard glare, trying to psyche him out. We eyed each other. I had had more experience as a leader and had learned how to control mutinous members with one steely glance. They had known that if they ever wanted to challenge my authority, they would have to fight me. And I boasted a reputation as a very good fighter. I was prepared to fight now. Panamania didn't make a move. I, too, held my ground.

"Nah," Panamania finally said, backing down. The moment of tension passed. Inwardly I sighed. He had had a switchblade; I had only my fists, having turned all my weapons over to the police. I would have to see Tarzan about getting me a switchblade.

"You can be vice-president," I told him generously. He shrugged but seemed mollified. He sat down on the grass again and took a long swig of wine. My leadership was now taken for granted. I was president of the MauMaus once again.

One evening a few weeks later, the MauMaus gathered in the park to get ready for a gang war with the Demons. There was an expectant excitement in the air. The boys milled about, psyching each other up, collecting weapons wrapped in newspaper and plastic bags, which had been hidden under chunks of grass. They examined them in anticipation—baseball bats, zipguns, brass knuckles, broomsticks, pipes, switchblades, chains, and machetes—before they passed them over to the girls for transport. At my signal, everyone split into small groups and headed for Demon turf, each group taking a different route.

I walked by myself. As a leader, I had to be something of a loner. To maintain my authority and respect, I had to remain aloof from the others. I couldn't get close to anybody; I had to stand alone.

In my mind, I went over the last rumbles we had had, and frowned. Something strange had come over me since I had come back to the gang. Outwardly I was still the same. It was my nature to be closed and secretive, which usually passed for being cool.

I still fought as hard as ever, but somehow it wasn't the old Israel who was fighting. Inwardly I had changed. For the past four years, fighting had been my whole life. It had given me my thrills, but now, for some strange reason, a lot of the joy I derived from it had disappeared. Now, whenever I thrust my knife into a guy's gut with a bitter vengeance, instead of the old rush of exhilaration, I was left with nothing but a hollow feeling in the pit of my stomach. And even worse, afterward I felt a twinge of guilt for what I had done. I knew it was wrong. I didn't share my private thoughts with anybody. The gang wouldn't understand what I was going through, anyway.

FOUR
Dead Hit

On Monday, February 23, 1959, five months
after I had turned my back on God, I left my
apartment and headed for my buddy Chino's
place.

Outside it was a cold, clear evening. A bitter
wind whipped against my thin leather jacket,
pressing against my rib cage like the dull steel
edge of a switchblade. I pulled my alpine hat
down low over my brow, turned up my collar,
gangster style, in a effort to shield my ears, and
shoved my gloved hands deep into my pockets in
a fistlike clench. Briskly, I walked along St.
Edward Street. The pavement beneath my feet
glistened as I passed under each street light.

I had no idea then, as I hurried along the
shabby streets of Ft. Greene, that the events of
the next few hours would profoundly change my
life. How could I know that this night would be

burned forever in my mind; that I would never be able to forget it?

So far, this evening promised to be much like any other. A few of the MauMaus had arranged to meet in the little city park next to Chino's apartment building. We called ourselves the Suicide Squad; we were a select group, a gang within a gang—the toughest core. Tonight we were out for a little excitement. For the last few days, a snowstorm had kept us cooped up indoors and now, bored and restless, we were eager to get together once again. We had no special plans for the evening; we were just going to hang around and talk and maybe go looking for trouble, or as we called it, jitter-bugging. And when we, the Suicide Squad, went looking for trouble, we usually found it—plenty.

Now, as I approached the city park on Monument Walk, which at this time of year was nothing but a patch of sooty snow overshadowed by towering apartment buildings, I could see that Carlos and Melvin had arrived before me. They were standing under a street light on the edge of the park. A fine mist of snow shimmered in the light above them as they stood absorbed in a serious conversation. Carlos was doing most of the talking: I could see the fog of his breath as he spoke. Mel had his head cocked to one side and was absently kicking a snowbank while he listened, adding the occasional profane word or two.

"Yeah, he's hurt bad," I overheard Carlos mutter to Mel as I walked up behind them. "His face is a mess. All black and blue. His jaw is busted and his eyes are swollen shut. A real ugly sight."

"Hey, man," I interrupted him, "what's this all about? Who's hurt?"

"Tico," Carlos told me grimly. "They jumped him last night. Beat him up real bad."

"Who did?" I demanded fiercely.

"The Sand Street Angels, those sons of—."

I swore. The Angels were an Italian gang whose turf bordered ours. It was rumored that they had connections with the Mafia, and they used this reputation to intimidate other gangs. This wasn't the first time we had had a run-in with them. There had been bad blood between us for a long time.

"Why'd they jump Tico?" I asked crossly. "What did he do?"

"Aw, you know Tico," Carlos shrugged. "He was messing around with their leader's sister. Couldn't keep his hands to himself."

I knew Tico, all right. He was a tough little guy, dark as an Indian, a born troublemaker. A real jitter-bugger. In this case, he probably deserved the beating; but deserved or not, such action demanded revenge. The Angels had openly challenged us. Our retaliation would be swift. We hadn't won our reputation as the most feared gang in Brooklyn by forgiving our enemies.

"Let's go look for those punks," I told Carlos and Mel. "When someone touches one of my boys, it's time to kill."

"Cool," Mel's eyes danced in his head, as they did whenever he was excited. "Let's bebop over to Angel turf right now and even up the score.

Pow!" He smashed one fist into the palm of his other hand. "We'll rock their jaws."

"I can dig that," Carlos agreed soberly. He had a caved-in face: his forehead and chin stuck out, but his nose was flattened and twisted, broken again and again in rumbles. "We'll show those filthy Wops that nobody messes with a MauMau and lives to tell about it."

"Yeah, baby," Mel grinned idiotically. "Before the night's over, those jerks'll be bending spaghetti in the grave." He guffawed with delight at that mental image and slapped Carlos' palm.

Chino joined us just then. He was fairly new to the gang, a natural athlete who spent more time working out in the gym than he did hanging around with us. He was a tall, good-looking Puerto Rican, but his Oriental appearance, his slanted eyes, his pale skin, and his straight, blue-black hair had earned him his nickname. "Hey, man, what's happening?" he asked.

I filled him in quickly. Chino listened, his face an expressionless mask. His hat, pulled down low over his brow, shadowed his eyes; only his prominent cheekbones, his square clean-cut jaw, caught the light. When I had finished speaking, he slipped his hand under his jacket and produced a .22 automatic. It lay like a dead weight in the palm of his hand, gleaming menacingly in the street light. "This'll teach those jacks a lesson," he said quietly.

"Cool, baby. All right!" Mel exclaimed in appreciation. "Where'd you get it?"

Chino shrugged, "Off an M.P." The Brooklyn

Navy Yard was located on the waterfront just behind the housing projects. He had been snooping around the docks when he had spotted the deserted military police car. With nobody in sight, he had ducked his head through the window, searched the glove compartment, and stashed the automatic under his jacket in a matter of seconds. Chino was very fast with his hands.

"Those punks'll listen to that, all right," Carlos murmured.

"Yeah, baby." Mel nodded his head, moving to his own inner beat. "Blood's gonna spill tonight. And it ain't gonna be ours." He was anxious to go. He was wild and crazy, sick in the head, the kind of guy who would smash a bottle in another guy's face without a moment's hesitation. It was rumored that his whole family was insane, and knowing Melvin, I could easily believe it.

"Well, what are we waiting for? Let's go get those chumps." I waved the gang forward. As we started down the block, Maximo, a dark-skinned, frizzy-haired boy from the Dominican Republic, joined us. The five of us, all Suicide Squad members, set off in search of the Angels. Only Tarzan was missing from the action tonight. And Nicky. But, of course, Nicky didn't count anymore. He was no longer one of us.

We knew where we could find the Sand Street boys. Their favorite hangout was the D and E Amusement Palace, a small penny arcade on the Flatbush Avenue Extension, about a mile and a half away. We headed in that direction now, cutting down deserted back streets. On this cold winter evening, everybody seemed to be holed up in apartments trying to keep warm. Only when we reached the tenement district on the edge of Ft. Greene did we pass a couple of winos sharing a bottle wrapped in a paper bag, and a few pathetic junkies crouched on their front steps, completely out of it. Everybody else had enough sense to get in out of the cold.

The five of us prowled the streets, like lean, hungry wolves stalking our prey, ready for the supreme moment . . . the kill. We wanted blood for blood.

I fingered the handle of the long hunting knife stuck in my belt. The blade was over a foot long and sharp, very sharp. By coincidence, Tico had been with me the day I had stolen it from a department store. He had been my lookout, keeping a sharp eye on the cashier, while I had casually taken the knife from its display shelf, and at the right moment, had slipped it into my belt. Now I was itching to stick the blade into an Angel's gut, in revenge for Tico's brutal beating. It seemed somehow fitting.

We turned onto Flatbush Avenue Extension, a busy, brightly lit eight-lane avenue, and walked the three long blocks to the D and E Amusement Palace. We were on enemy turf now, but we walked down the street like we owned it—doing the slow easy walk of the jitter-bug, loosely swinging our shoulders, hips, and knees, bobbing and weaving to our own individual rhythm, tapping our bamboo canes in front of us.

Shortly after eight o'clock, we arrived at the D and E Amusement Palace. Inside, sixty pinball machines were crammed side by side into the long narrow building. Tonight appeared to be a slow night for business. Only a few guys were playing the machines, and none of them were Angels. Except one.

"Hey, you," I called to a mean-looking youth who was leaning against a pinball machine, sipping a coke. I had recognized him as the Angel who worked in this joint. He was here to keep an eye on things, so customers wouldn't be tempted to unscrew the machine moneyboxes and make off with their contents.

"Yeah, whadya want?" He knew who we were, all right, but he stared at us insolently and continued to sip on his coke.

"Hey, man, where's your leader at?" I kept my hand resting lightly on my belt, next to my knife.

"He ain't here right now," he answered glibly. "Whadya want him for?"

"Real nosy dude, ain't he?" I said to my boys. I chewed on my big wad of gum, and then cracked it loudly. "Don't you worry what we want him for. We just want a little talk, that's all."

"Well, he'll be here in a little while," the Angel drawled lazily, "but if you dudes hang around any longer, you're all gonna be dead."

Mel's switchblade clicked open. "Wanna be the first to go, wise boy?" He wanted to do the Angel in right then and there. I restrained him.

"Not now, Mel. He ain't the guy we want."

Mel scowled, but his hand dropped limply to his side. He couldn't resist adding, "If you don't shut your mouth, man, you're gonna eat your teeth."

The Angel shrugged. "If you dudes ain't gonna play the machines, you'd better scram. This is a place of business. We don't want no trouble in here." He glanced around at the other boys in the place, as if mutely asking for their support. They had all stopped playing by now, and were watching us dumbly. No one dared to move.

"C'mon," I told my boys, "let's wait outside."

Before long we were numb with cold and stamped our frozen feet to keep the blood circulating.

"What's keeping those jerks?" Carlos muttered impatiently. He threw down his cigarette and stamped on it.

"Yeah, this ain't no fun," grumbled Melvin. "I want some action."

"Aw, they'll be here soon. Don't worry," I told them.

"Yeah, we can wait," Maximo grinned. "We've got all night."

Twenty minutes later, we saw the Angels coming up over the hill. Chino, with eyes like a cat, had spotted them first. We watched them jitter-bugging down the sloped avenue toward us, laughing and joking, taking their time. The adrenaline started to flow through my body. I was keyed up, tense, ready for anything.

"OK, guys," I half whispered. "Stay cool. We won't make a move until they do."

"Yeah," Carlos agreed, "but if they start something, we finish it."

The Angels stopped ten feet away from us,

forming a tight semicircle. They were wearing coffee-colored trench coats with the collars turned up, and dark felt hats. Two of the eight had dark sunglasses on—they were probably high on drugs.

The Angel leader, a tall, muscle-bound youth, very broad in the shoulders, stepped forward. His hands hung loosely by his side, a cigarette dangled from his lip. "Hey, what you doing on our turf? You don't belong around here."

I stepped forward to face him. I, too, kept my hands free, ready at any moment to rip out my knife. All of us had weapons concealed somewhere on our bodies. "We came to talk to you, man. We want to know how come you dudes were tramping one of our boys?"

The Angel leader took a long drag on his cigarette and exhaled the smoke in my face. "That ain't none of your business, man."

"Well, we're making it our business. Dig it?"

"So what's there to talk about?" he sneered.

"Like I said, man," I controlled my temper, fighting to keep my cool. "How come you messed up our boy?"

The leader swore and threw his cigarette away in disgust. "So he got messed up a little. So what?" he said sarcastically, an obvious challenge in his tone.

I could see that talking wasn't getting us anywhere. It was time to cut the small talk. Fists would do all the talking now, in a language we all understood. I eyed him lazily, "Maybe you wanna get jacked up right now, huh?"

"Cool. Let's get it on."

We stared at each other, daring the other one to make the first move. All this time, the two gangs had been inching imperceptibly closer to each other, until now less than a yard separated us. Overhead, the neon lights blinked on and off.

Suddenly, out of the corner of my eye, I saw a burly Angel, standing on the fringe of his group, take a swing at Maximo. We had a name for this kind of sneak attacker—"Jap-artist," in memory of Pearl Harbor. Luckily, Maximo ducked his head, taking the full impact of the blow on his shoulder. He staggered backward momentarily, but after quickly regaining his balance, smashed the Angel square in the jaw. Maximo, who lifted weights, packed a mighty wallop. The Angel crumpled to the pavement, and before he could get up, Maximo lunged on top of him. They rolled on the ground, fighting furiously.

Chino, who had remained stolidly silent throughout the proceedings, now stepped up beside me. Though his eyes were shaded under the rim of his hat, I knew they had narrowed to a slit.

"Hey, man, we ought to blow you away," he said in a low voice, the hidden automatic giving him a quiet confidence. I let him take over. It was up to him, now; he had the gun.

The Angel leader snorted in contempt. "Yeah, sure. You guys ain't got no guts. You're a bunch of chickens. You ain't gonna do nothin'," he egged Chino on. The leader was cocky, self-assured. Too cocky.

"Yeah?" Chino said in the same even, quietly modulated voice. He was taller than the Angel leader, built like a basketball player with the same litheness of movement. He slipped the .22 automatic from his belt and pointed it carelessly at the leader. Then, in a flat voice that held no hint of passion, he said calmly, deliberately.

"Like I said, man. I'm gonna blow you away."

The leader attempted to laugh, but no laugh came. "You stinkin' Spic," he spit on the ground.

Something snapped inside Chino. He had been pushed too far. He raised the automatic, aiming it steadily at the leader's eyes. "Goodbye," he said softly and pulled the trigger. He was less than two feet away.

The leader slumped to the ground. He lay where he had fallen, unmoving. A pool of blood formed on the pavement around his head. Blood poured in a thick rich stream from his nose, his eyes, his ears, and down the side of his mouth. No one moved.

Chino stared blankly at the body of the fallen youth. Then he raised the .22 again and shot him in the chest. An ugly dark stain spread rapidly over the top half of the boy's trenchcoat. Half-crazed, Chino then turned the automatic on the Angels. One boy yelped in pain as a bullet tore through the flesh of his hand and shattered the glass front of the Amusement Palace behind him. The Angels fled.

"C'mon, let's get out of here," I yelled to the others. I had only then become aware of the gaping people scattered all over the street. They were standing frozen in horror. No one screamed, no one tried to stop us.

We ducked down DeKalb Avenue, running for

all we were worth in the direction of our own turf. We were fast runners—we had had a lot of practice. Chino stopped once to drop the automatic down a sewer grate. I threw away my hunting knife as we passed an empty lot. The others also ditched their weapons somewhere along the way.

When we had run five long blocks, we finally slowed to a walk, gasping for breath. We laughed and whooped and slapped each other on the palms, feeling lightheaded and slightly hysterical.

"Man, we sure got those Wops this time!" cried Carlos.

"Yeah, we burned them good," agreed Chino.

"Dig us. We're the Lone Rangers," exclaimed Melvin gleefully.

We all burst into a fresh fit of laughter. It was then that I noticed that Maximo wasn't with us. "Hey, where's Maximo?"

"Beats me," Carlos shrugged. "He was right behind me two minutes ago."

"Guess he must've taken a wrong turn," I said, dismissing it.

"Yeah," Mel grinned, "he'll catch up."

But he didn't, and we never saw him again.

Ahead of us we could see the towering apartment complex of the Ft. Greene Projects. Our turf. We were almost safe now, almost home free. We walked almost drunkenly down the street, feeling high from the fresh sweet taste of our latest victory.

"That'll teach those jacks to mess around with us," Carlos laughed scornfully.

"Yeah, man. We're the greatest!"

FIVE
Red-handed

We had almost reached the intersection of Myrtle
Avenue and Ashland Place, when without warning, two squad cars squealed around the corner
behind us. We didn't have time to run. Before
we realized what was happening, the first squad
car had pulled up onto the curb, blocking the
sidewalk in front of us, while the second had cut
us off from behind. We were trapped in the
middle: there was no escape.

A policeman jumped out of the car in front of
us.

"Put your hands up," he ordered, pointing a
gun at us. He was holding the revolver with both
hands to steady his aim, but his hands were
shaking. After seeing what had taken place on
Flatbush Avenue, he didn't know whether we
would try to shoot our way clear or not.

We raised our hands in surrender. With a .38
special aimed at my face, I wasn't going to argue.

To make a run for it now would be suicidal. One thing that I had never believed was that cops shot their guns off into the air; I didn't want to give this particular cop any target practice. The four of us stood there facing him, hands above our heads, bathed in the blood-red flashing light of his squad car.

"All right, boys, up against the car," the second policeman directed us from behind. "Put your hands on the roof and spread your legs apart. Move it!" With his free hand he shoved us against the side of the car. He trained his revolver on our backs while the first cop frisked us. Of course, he found no weapons on us. At least we had had enough time to dump them.

"They're clean," he said. He grabbed my arms and pinned them behind my back, snapping handcuffs on my wrists. I winced at the feel of cold steel against my flesh.

I was pushed into the back seat of the squad car. Then the door on the other side opened and Mel stumbled in beside me. Chino and Carlos were herded into the other car. A screen separated us from the policeman in the front seat, as he backed the car up. As we sped down the block, sirens screaming, Mel and I exchanged glances in the darkness and shrugged.

It wasn't the first time that we had shared the back seat of a squad car. Many times after rumbles, the police had picked us up for questioning, especially when serious injuries were involved. Sometimes they had driven us to the precinct, but other times they had just taken us for a spin around the block, trying to scare us. During those occasions, they had never been able to charge us with a crime. When fifty or sixty boys are fighting each other, it's difficult to prove who had been responsible for one boy's fatal stab wounds or another's beating. They had never been able to prove anything against us before, but this time, I had the feeling, it was going to be different. At least Maximo had been lucky enough to escape.

We were whisked to the nearest police station, on Poplar Street. I had been in and out of this station's doors many times. Just last month I had been brought here for questioning about my involvement in a fight. But it was funny to think that the second to last time I had been in a police station, I had walked in voluntarily. That was when I had turned over all my weapons to the police after I had become a Christian. Now I had been arrested for murder. A chasm separated that day and this one.

After our names, addresses, and fingerprints were recorded, all four of us were locked in the holding tank. This wasn't new to me either. I had been temporarily locked up while waiting to be questioned before, but always I had been let go after a few hours. Usually the police had phoned my mother to come and pick me up. On those occasions she had been very angry with me, and told me to behave myself. But I had just let her scolding go in one ear and out the other.

In the holding tank, we paced back and forth, trying not to get into each other's way. There were no benches in the cell, so we were forced to stand.

"Man, why did we stop running?" Mel fumed. "Just a few more blocks and we would have been safe!" The scars on his forehead stood out more than usual.

"Yeah," I agreed gloomily. "If only we had kept on running. . . . But, man, those bulls came out of nowhere. They sure picked us up fast."

"If only we had seen them before it was too late. . . ." Carlos rubbed his thumb against his flattened nose. "We didn't stand a chance."

In the large empty room in front of us, there was a sudden commotion. I peered through the bars, trying to see what was going on.

"Hey, man, what's happening?" Carlos asked me. The others joined me at the bars.

"Aw, its just the Angels," I told him. "Jerks!"

Six of the Sand Street Angels had just entered the room, escorted by a policeman. When they saw us behind the bars, they shouted across the room: "Yeah, those are the ones!"

"They did it!"

"They killed him!"

They tried to rush over to the holding tank, but the policeman restrained them. He told them to sit down on the bench in front of the questioning room.

"We're going to get you," an Angel snarled.

"Yeah, just you wait, man . . ." another threatened.

We laughed.

"How you gonna catch us, man?" I sneered. "We're safe here."

"We're gonna send you filthy Spics away for

good," another Angel cried. "We're gonna make sure you pay for knockin' off Tony!"

"Yeah, baby," Mel sassed them back, "we burned him good!"

"We're gonna make sure you dudes are gonna get the electric chair!" they hissed.

"They're just blowing steam," I whispered to the others. "Don't pay them no mind. Keep cool."

We just laughed at the Angels' threats. The more we laughed, the angrier the Angels got. The guard let them shout at us, but he wouldn't let them near the bars. One by one they were taken into the other room for questioning. After awhile everything settled down. I stared through the bars glumly. I could laugh at the Angels, but we were behind bars and they weren't.

"You know, those boys over there may be right," the policeman guarding us told me. "You four are in big trouble. You could be facing the electric chair. . . ."

I shrugged. If he was trying to frighten me, he wasn't succeeding. I stretched my hands through the bars, interlocked my fingers, and cracked my knuckles.

A half an hour later, the sergeant took a break from his questioning. He came out to get himself a hot chocolate from the vending machine by the far wall.

"Hey, Gus. Ask the boys if they want some," he called over, before returning to his room.

The guard turned around to face us. "You guys thirsty?"

"Yeah, man!" We all nodded vigorously. It

was cold in the cell. Very cold. We hadn't noticed it at first, but now the reaction had set in. At least they had allowed us to keep our jackets.

The guard came back and handed us each a styrofoam cup of hot chocolate. We sipped it gratefully and had a smug bit of satisfaction in knowing that the Angels had to pay for their own. But if the cops thought a warm drink would loosen our tongues, they had another thing coming. Our turn for interrogation would be next.

The four of us moved to the back of the holding tank and held a conference in hushed tones.

"Look, man, we've got to discuss what we're gonna tell the 'bulls,'" I told the others. "We've got to get it straight."

"Yeah, we've all got to take the rap," Carlos said. "We're in this together." We respected Carlos. He was the oldest among us—seventeen—and sometimes took over the leadership.

"Right." Chino slapped Carlos' palm. "I can dig that."

"And no matter what, we don't squeal on Maximo," I went on. "If they ask us about him, we don't say nothin'. Understand?"

"Right."

"Got it."

"And if they ask who fired the shots—we don't know nothing. OK?"

"Cool," everyone agreed, especially Chino.

Carlos was called out for questioning first. We all waited anxiously for him to come back.

"How'd it go, man?" we asked.

"No sweat. They couldn't squeeze nothin' out of me," Carlos said confidently.

When Chino had gone for his turn, I asked Carlos, "Do you think we can beat this rap?" I respected his opinion.

"No chance," Carlos said glumly. "They've got too much proof. Too many witnesses." He ran his fingers thoughtfully through his curly hair.

"Yeah," I sighed, cracking my knuckles. "Things don't look too good. How much time do you figure we're gonna get?"

"For murder? Who knows?" Carlos threw up his hands.

I was next. A policeman escorted me across the room to the sergeant's office. The Angels were no longer seated on the bench; they had all gone home.

Inside the small room, the sergeant was seated behind his desk, sipping another cup of hot chocolate with great concentration. The transcriber sat to his left, pen poised and ready to write. The sergeant indicated the other chair and I sat down. The cop remained standing behind me, acting as a witness. Immediately, the sergeant fired questions at me:

"What happened?"

"Who had the gun?"

"Who did the shooting?"

I shrugged. "I dunno," I replied to most of his questions, playing it dumb. I wasn't going to cooperate with any cops. I kept my mouth shut.

"All right, who was the fifth guy that was with you?" the sergeant changed his line of questioning.

"What other guy? There was nobody else—just the four of us."

"No, there were five of you," the sergeant repeated stubbornly. "Now tell me this guy's name."

"I dunno what you're talking about, man! I told you there were only four of us and you've got us all here."

"C'mon, Narvaez. Witnesses say there were five of you. . . ."

"Well, if that's so, I dunno who the other guy was."

"You mean to tell me," the sergeant said scornfully, "that you hang around with this guy and you don't know his name!"

"We don't know who he was. We never saw him before," I said sweetly. He couldn't crack me. It was against gang code to rat on one another.

I could see that the sergeant was getting tired. All the resistance he had met this evening was wearing him out. Now he tried a different tactic. He reverted back to the killing.

"C'mon, Narvaez. Open up. Who had the gun?"

I shrugged. The sergeant was wasting his time.

"Look, you may as well come clean. Chino's already admitted that he did the shooting."

I wasn't falling for that line. "Well, good for him. I dunno who did it."

The sergeant sighed.

"All right, call in Chino," the sergeant told the policeman. A few minutes later, Chino was brought in. We made a face at one another.

"OK, Chino. Tell us once more what you've already admitted. I want Narvaez here to hear it—right from your own mouth. Did you shoot and kill the Sand Street Angel, Chino?"

Chino looked at me, then hung his head. "Yeah, it was me," he confessed glumly. "I done it."

"Is that what you say, Narvaez?" the sergeant turned to me. "Do you agree?"

"Yeah," I said quietly. "He's telling the truth."

"OK, good. That's what we want to hear. Take them back to the tank, Bernie," the sergeant told the policeman, dismissing us.

We waited in silence in the holding tank. Chino was taken out again to show the police where he had dropped the .22 automatic down the sewer grate. A half hour later, we were packed into the squad car once again.

"Now where are they taking us?" I asked myself without curiosity. I felt like an animal being herded around. "Well, man, I don't care where they take me—just as long as I can hit the sack." I was dead tired. I slumped against the back seat and stared blindly at the passing shadowed buildings and neon signs. They hypnotized me; my eyelids felt heavy. The squad car cruised down the silent, deserted streets. It was after 3 A.M.

The squad car stopped in front of a building that had most of its lights on. We piled out and the policeman escorted us into a medium-sized room with ten rows of empty benches on either side of the aisle. Now I knew where we were— night court. We filed down the aisle to the front of the courtroom where we were made to stand beneath the judge's bench.

Finally the judge, in his long black robes, entered the room from a side door and mounted the steps to his bench. He sat down, peering over the rim of his glasses, silently inspecting the four of us. We shuffled our feet and grinned at each other. No judge was going to intimidate us. He ordered us to stand up straight and we complied—for about five minutes. Then we slouched once again, looking at the ceiling, at the floor—anywhere but at the judge.

"C'mon, man," I silently urged the judge, "let's get this over with. . . ." I was fed up with the whole business.

The judge read out the charge against us. It sounded like a bunch of mumble-jumble to me; I didn't even listen. Instead, I shifted my weight from one foot to the other and concentrated on a crack in the wall. My wrists itched from the handcuffs; I longed to scratch them. I knew that if the judge kept us here much longer I would burst out laughing at any minute. I felt strangely detached from the scene; it seemed like some kind of bizarre joke to me.

Then the judge finally said something that I understood: he arraigned us with the charge of premeditated murder.

"Big deal," I thought to myself. "Who cares?"

The four of us grinned at each other. I winked at Chino. We were in the big time now.

The judge scowled. He informed us that there had been an outrageous number of gang killings that year; it had to be stopped. We got the feeling he was going to use our case as an example.

We snickered. We were cool.

"Man, you can't scare us," I scoffed inwardly. Later, however, I would have a lot of time to think about the judge's warning.

The police shuffled us out of the courtroom. Outside on the steps, a pack of reporters threw questions at us. Flashbulbs exploded in our faces. The reporters had got wind of the gang murder and had trailed us from the police station to the night court. We clowned around for the photographers; we didn't mind getting our pictures taken.

"We've made the news," I gloated. "Tomorrow morning we'll be on the front page of all the papers . . . that's something." But I didn't like the way the reporters were bombarding us with questions.

"How do you feel?" one reporter asked, dodging in front of me.

"I don't feel nothin'," I snapped. "What am I supposed to feel, man?"

"Have you anything to say about the killing?" another reporter pursued me.

"It's no big deal. If I had had the gun I would have killed them all!"

"Why did you do it?" another tried to block me.

"Get out of my face," I hissed, ignoring his question. I wanted to slug him in the face, but the handcuffs prevented me. At that moment, I was full of hatred for everyone. I wanted to strike out at all the inquisitive faces around me.

"Leave me alone," I wanted to scream, "just leave me alone."

The police escorted us to the squad car. I climbed into the back seat, as the reporters continued to snap pictures through the window and crowded around the car. I was relieved when we sped off into the night. I had no idea where they were taking me, but I didn't care. I'd roll with the punches.

The evening's events blurred in my mind. I rested my chin on my chest. An enormous weight settled on my shoulders and pushed me down, down, down. I felt myself sinking into oblivion.

SIX
The Cage

"OK, boys, out."

We had stopped in front of an imposing, modern eight-story building on Atlantic Avenue. It was a long, narrow structure, mainly glass with a thin strip of white brick running down the sides. Each level was dimly lit by a few hall lights. I had walked by this building many times before, and although nothing about its appearance betrayed its purpose, I knew what it was; I had never thought I would end up on the inside one day. Now I was too tired to fully comprehend what was happening to me.

The Atlantic Detention Home was open for arrivals at all hours of the day and night. The four policemen herded us across the sidewalk up the steps to the entrance. When Mel turned to say something to me, the nearest policeman shoved him along. "Keep moving," he ordered.

The policeman at the head of the procession

rang the bell beside the door, while we waited in line behind him. A guard in a gold-buttoned blue uniform, reaching for a large ring of keys around his belt, opened the door for us. We trooped inside.

The main reception room was a cold, empty room with no furniture in it and a row of cells all around it. Four more guards met us. Our handcuffs were removed. I rubbed my wrists, wincing as the blood began to freely circulate—and then our fingerprints and mug shots were taken for the detention home's own files. We were ordered not to talk to one another.

"All right. Everyone strip!"

That woke me up. I undressed slowly; inside I was furious. I was being stripped of more than my clothes, I was being stripped of my rights.

"I don't take my clothes off for nobody!" I fumed, highly indignant. As president of the MauMaus, I had been giving orders for so long, it was hard to get used to taking them myself.

Standing naked and defenseless, I tensed as a guard searched my body thoroughly for hidden drugs or weapons.

"Bend over," he commanded me, checking my private parts.

"You dirty cracker," I cursed him under my breath. I loathed the idea of being naked in front of other men; I had heard stories of what could happen.

A young inmate entered the room and sprayed us with a disinfectant from a milk can. Another guard routinely checked through our clothes, turning the pockets of our leather jackets and dungarees inside out. Finding nothing, he threw our clothes back to us and we were finally allowed to get dressed again.

The lieutenant walked into the room and looked us over. I could tell by the stiff way he moved that he wasn't a very happy person. He had a stern Nordic face, blond hair chopped into a severe crewcut, and was wearing a blue uniform like the other guards, but he had gold bars beneath the collar. He introduced himself. His welcoming speech was brief and to the point:

"I want to make sure that you young men clearly understand the rules of this detention center," he bellowed. "If you obey your instructions and behave yourselves, there'll be no problems. But if, on the other hand, you step out of line," he warned us, "you'll have to suffer the consequences. We do not tolerate troublemakers here. Is that understood?" He examined each of our faces in turn, checking for any hint of rebellion.

We all nodded solemnly. We got the message. Of course, I didn't intend to take him too seriously—I was prepared to fight if the need arose.

"Good. Take them to their cells," he dismissed us. One of the guards stepped forward and led us over to the elevators. Along the way, we were handed a pair of blankets and sheets. Inside the elevator, the four of us grinned at each other behind the guard's back. He wasn't armed and we weren't handcuffed, but there was no place to run.

On the fifth floor, we went our separate ways.

Another guard on duty took Mel and Carlos to the left block of cells while Chino and I were taken to the right. Chino was locked up in his cell and then I was taken around to the other side of the cellblock. The guard escorted me up the steel-grilled stairs to the upper level of cells. At the master switch control box, he pressed a button to electronically open a cell. I heard the telltale and terrifying click as the cell door popped open.

"Go to cell number 18," he instructed me, making no move to follow me. "Third cell over."

I walked down the narrow two-foot-wide wooden catwalk in front of the row of cells. In the first cell, I passed a sleeping Negro boy, and in the second, a Puerto Rican who was tossing and turning feverishly on his cot. The third cell was empty, the door slightly ajar. I pulled it back, stepped into the cell, and then grated the door shut behind me. It locked automatically.

"What have I got myself into?" I groaned. The click of the cell door locking had sounded so final. For a moment I stood by the door, paralyzed. The cell before me was ten feet by six feet. I could spread my arms and touch both of the side walls at the same time. The faint light of dawn filtering in through the windows behind me cast a dull gleam on the toilet bowl and sink in one corner of the cell; in the other corner was a cot.

I walked over to the cot and tossed my blankets and sheets on the end, not bothering to unfold them. I sat on the edge of the bed, holding my head in my hands. The mattress was only four inches thick; I could feel the tightly coiled steel springs beneath me.

I don't know how long I sat like that. When I looked up, I found a guard watching me. He passed on. The guard's catwalk was twenty feet away, across the cavernous space in front of my bars. It was positioned halfway between the two levels, so that the patrolling guards could keep a watchful eye on both the upper and lower levels at the same time. Behind the guard's catwalk, the thick plastic windows allowed the light to enter the cells, but gave a distorted view of the street below.

"What have I got myself into?" I repeated again, dazed. It was no joke. For once in my life, I was worried, very worried. I looked around my cell, catching sight of my own dim reflection in the wall across from me. The walls were slabs of steel and were painted a high gloss, hospital-green.

"I wonder if Mom's worried about me?" I thought to myself. "Maybe she doesn't even know I'm missing. Maybe she thinks I'm sleeping safely in my own bed. . . ."

Somewhere, someone coughed. I was acutely conscious of the heavy breathing and snoring of the inmates all around me. The Puerto Rican in the next cell over moaned without ceasing. He sounded like he was in pain.

"Just my luck to be next to a sissy," I muttered. "He's probably got a tummyache and wants his mommy!"

In the distance I heard the muffled sound of an engine turning over, and then an ambulance siren. As my cell grew lighter, the traffic on Atlantic Avenue picked up. The hustle and bustle of the awakening outside world seemed very far away.

I sat on my bed, staring absently through the bars, quietly watching the dawn. I don't know what I was waiting for—morning, perhaps. Every half hour the guards patrolled their beat. I could hear the jangling of their keys and the creaking of the catwalk before they came into sight. Their footsteps echoed hollowly on the wooden boards as they passed, then faded.

For some reason I couldn't sleep.

"Man, you'll have plenty of time to sleep," I kidded myself mockingly. "That's all there is to do here—sleep."

After six o'clock, I heard the sounds of the other inmates awakening: taps running and toilets flushing. Finally, at quarter to seven, the buzzer rang for everyone to get up. Further down the cell block, boys were shouting obscenities to each other, joking and laughing, and somewhere on the level below, somebody was whistling an irritating tune. I stood up and stretched and then walked over to the sink and splashed my face with cold water. I cupped my hands, bent over, and drank some cold water. Above the sink, a slab of aluminum acted as a makeshift mirror; glass was not allowed in the cells—it was too dangerous. I peered at my vague, distorted image and combed my hair.

At seven o'clock, all the cell doors clicked open and the inmates slid them back far enough to pass through. I stepped out on the catwalk and followed the Negro boy in front of me. The Puerto Rican boy remained in his cell, writhing on his bed, his clothing and sheets soaked with sweat.

"If he wants to miss breakfast, that's his problem," I shrugged, passing his cell. "But, man, am I starved!"

We filed down the steel-grilled stairs to the level below. In the open area, catering wagons had been set up to serve breakfast. Three inmates stood behind each wagon dishing out steaming bowls of oatmeal or cornflakes. I picked up a stainless steel tray and joined the meal line. When my turn came, I chose the oatmeal. I felt like having something hot; it had been cold in the cell. I carried my tray over to the Day Room, which at mealtimes was transformed into a mess hall, and passed the guard who stood to one side of the entrance. Inside the door, I hesitated for a moment, searching for a familiar face. About twenty boys were spread across the room, seated at six long tables. At one of them, I spotted Melvin and Carlos, already digging into their cereal. They waved me over.

"How's it goin', man?" I greeted them cheerily, sliding one leg over the bench.

"OK," Mel mumbled, his mouth stuffed with oatmeal. He looked unkempt this morning, which was his usual state. His hair was tousled, his chin unshaven, and his shirttail sticking out of his dungarees.

"Did you get any sleep?" I asked him.

"Nah," Mel shrugged. He looked at me with bleary red eyes. "But what else is new?"

"Me neither," I laughed. "Dig them crazy cages!"

"Yeah," Carlos said dryly, "the Hilton this ain't." He seemed in unusually good spirits this morning.

"I'm starved," I announced, attacking my bowl of oatmeal. "Yech!" I cried after I had gulped down a generous spoonful. "This stuff tastes like glue. . . ." I washed it down with a drink of milk.

Mel guffawed. "I could have warned you, but I wanted to see your face." He pounded the table with his fist. I laughed in spite of myself. There was something about Melvin that made you laugh.

"Tomorrow," Carlos said, agreeing with my culinary opinion, "I'm having cornflakes."

"Whatsamatter? You too good for this joint?" Mel teased him. "You guys better get used to that junk."

"Well, it's free, anyhow," I joked. "Guess we can't complain. . . ."

"Hi, guys," Chino sat down. "What's happening?"

"We're dying of food poisoning, that's what," Carlos retorted.

"It's a better way to go than that Angel did," Chino commented dryly.

"Yeah, baby, that's right," Mel slapped Chino's palm. "Those Angels won't mess with us MauMaus again!"

"Dig it," Carlos remarked. "That Angel jerk is probably six feet under by now."

"Compared to where he's at," Chino shrugged,

looking around, "this joint ain't so bad."

"Our pictures should be in all the morning's papers," I reflected. "Bet we make the headlines."

"Cool. Our mugs'll be famous all over New York City," Carlos said.

"What do you mean—New York City?" Mel was aghast. "More like New York State!"

"Crazy, baby! We've hit the big time." I smiled, humoring Mel.

"I wonder what my old man's gonna say when he reads about us?" Carlos reflected. His mother had died a few years ago; all of his brothers and sisters more or less had brought up themselves. "I'll bet I can hear him hollering from here!"

"Yeah, I guess our folks know all about it by now," Chino said, lost within his own grim thoughts.

"My old lady's not goin' to take this thing very good," I said, suddenly wondering what my mother's reaction would be. I had never thought about it before. "She'll crack up."

"Aw, knock it off, you guys," Mel said in mock severity. "Who cares? I know my old man and lady ain't gonna care. Besides," he joked, "they never read the papers. They don't know what's goin' on half the time!"

"Mel, your folks are crazy anyway," Carlos half kidded him.

"Visiting hours are after supper," Chino remarked absently. "Guess we'll have to face the music tonight. . . ."

That evening after supper, a guard opened my cell door. "Someone's here to see you, Narvaez," he informed me, impassively. "You've got a visitor."

I jumped up. There was only one person in the whole world it could be . . . my mother! My father couldn't come, I knew, because he was away as usual on another voyage.

The guard escorted me to the special visiting room on the first floor. Fifteen booths, side by side, filled the room. I slipped into one and waited for my mother to come. The booth was much like an ordinary telephone booth, with a stool to sit on, a telephone on the wall, and a ten-by-six-inch pane of glass to look through to the booth on the other side.

A few minutes later my mother came and sat down opposite me. She had a handkerchief pressed to her mouth; the tears were spilling down her cheeks. She wouldn't meet my eyes. With her free hand she alternately clutched the large leather purse that threatened to fall off her lap, or fumbled jerkily at the nylon scarf knotted tightly at her neck, as if she found it hard to breathe. I looked at her helplessly through the small window. She seemed very frail and small and I could see that she was shaking. All at once, I wanted to reach out and touch her, comfort her in some way, but the partition was a barrier between us and there were other invisible barriers besides.

"Mom . . ." I said lamely, after picking up the telephone. It was all I could manage.

"Israel," she blubbered, "Oh, Israel!"

I waited for her to gain her composure. When she spoke finally, it was with great difficulty.

"Israel, are you all right?" She choked on the words. "Are you hurt?"

"Nah," I shrugged. "I'm OK."

"Are you sure?" she asked again anxiously.

"Yeah, Mom, I'm cool." I wanted to say more, but the words wouldn't come. "Why, she really cares about me," I thought. It was a revelation.

"Oh, Israel, Israel. What's happening to my boys?" she sobbed, speaking more to herself than to me. "Such good boys. . . ." She broke down again, covering her face with her hands.

For the first time, I had a chance to really study my mother. Before, I had hardly paid any attention to her; she had just always been part of the furniture. Now I could see that she was really suffering.

"What's happening to my boys?" she repeated again in a voice so low I barely caught the words. "First Benjamin and now you."

My mother was shocked and confused. She couldn't understand what was happening. I felt sorry for her. She had tried to raise us as best as she knew how, but with nine children to care for, it hadn't been easy. Now we were all turning out bad; we were constantly getting into trouble. Three years ago, my oldest brother Benjamin had spent a year in jail, and now I was in the same predicament. I had been too young then to understand what was going on and nobody had bothered to explain to me. Now I searched for words that would explain to my mother about my own situation. But what could I say? What would she understand?

"Are they feeding you OK?" my mother blurted out, wiping her face with the handkerchief. With an obvious effort, she pulled herself together.

"Yeah, the food's OK," I muttered, relieved that I had been rescued temporarily from an explanation. For the moment my mother was more concerned about my health than about the crime. Her protective maternal instinct had been aroused.

"Do you need anything?" she sniffed. "What can I bring you?" She was as practical as ever.

"Lots of stuff. More clothes—shirts, pants—everything, but especially underclothes."

"And what else?" she asked, eager to do something to help her son.

"My toothbrush, toothpaste, soap, cookies—whatever you can think of. . . ."

"OK, I'll bring them for you tomorrow. Oh, Israel," she shook her head, rocking back and forth on her stool. I was afraid that she was going to break down again. I couldn't stand to see her cry; it made me feel uncomfortable. "My poor boy. . . ."

"Don't worry, Mom," I told her lightly. "I'm OK."

"What happened?" she finally blurted out.

What could I tell her? I searched for gentle words, but couldn't find anything to soften the blow.

"We went looking for this guy—he'd beaten up a buddy of ours—and we killed him," I told her bluntly. "Just like that." I shrugged.

My mother must have suspected before that I was involved in the gangs. My frequent examinations by the police had made her suspicious. She had met many of the MauMaus—Nicky, Carlos, Chino, Tico, and others, when I had brought them to our apartment. I had just introduced them to her as my friends, and though she might have suspected otherwise, what could she say? She had warned me many times not to get involved with the gangs, but she didn't know how deeply I was already enmeshed with them. I had told her that these guys weren't gang members—they were just my school buddies.

My mother looked at me through swollen eyes. "Well, you didn't have nothing to do with it, did you?" She was reluctant to believe that her son could be involved in murder.

"I was just with these guys," I said.

"But you didn't do the shooting, did you?" she asked quickly.

"No. . . ."

"Oh," she sighed, immensely relieved. "In other words, you're just an accomplice."

"That's right."

"You're sure you're not hurt?" she asked for the hundredth time.

"Nah."

She sighed again, closing her eyes. "I heard all about it on the eleven o'clock news last night. I was so worried!"

"I'm all right, Mom," I repeated woodenly. What else could I say?

"Nobody's trying to say you shot the boy?" she inquired anxiously, a new thought suddenly occurring to her.

"No. Chino's confessed to doing it."

"Well, I'm gonna get you a good lawyer."

"Thanks, Mom." I didn't think it would do me any good.

"Now don't you worry about anything—"

"I'm cool."

Our time together was soon up. My mother rose slowly to her feet, dabbing at her eyes with her handkerchief.

"Goodbye, Israel."

"Catch you later, Mom."

I was genuinely sorry to see her leave. In the last half hour, I had felt closer to my mother than I had at any other time in the past sixteen years of my life. It hurt me to see her so broken—hurt me more than I would care to admit. I knew that it was my fault that she was suffering, but there was nothing I could do about it now. What I had done, I had done.

Feeling tense and frustrated, I followed the guard back to my cell, carrying those brief moments of my mother's visit back with me. It was all I had left.

SEVEN
Rumble

"I see number seventeen's gone."

Two guards were talking on the catwalk beneath me. I drew closer to the bars to listen in to their conversation.

"Yeah," the other guard remarked. "They took him away last night. He tried to electrocute himself."

That explained a lot of things to me. Last night I had had a restless sleep. The dope addict in the cell next to me had shaken his bars and pounded the walls, his moans turning into screams. He had desperately wanted a fix. The guards had done nothing to calm him down. Toward morning, I had heard shuffling in the next cell and then silence: the screaming had suddenly stopped. Later, when I had passed his cell on the way to breakfast, I had found it empty.

"Who was on duty?" one of the guards asked.

"Frank. He found the boy with one finger sticking into the light socket and one foot in water. He'd smashed the light covering with his shoe."

"Crazy guy!"

"Yeah, you have to watch these dope addicts. When they get desperate they'll try anything."

A few days later, when the young dope addict was returned to his cell, I tried to strike up a conversation with him.

"Hey, man, where you from?" I asked.

"Manhattan."

"What you get busted for?" I continued, already knowing his probable answer.

"Drug possession."

"Yeah, I figured. Heard you going through cold turkey."

He grunted. "Man, it was bad." He didn't mention the suicide attempt and neither did I.

"Where did they take you?"

"The hospital. They fixed me up OK."

"What they give you? Methadone?"

"Yeah, I guess. . . ."

"Feelin' better?"

"OK. I still feel shaky."

He wasn't very talkative. Most of the time, he was very moody and withdrawn. I talked with him on and off, but most of the conversation was one-sided. In fact, I often wondered if he had gone to sleep on me. By the next weekend, his trial came up and he was released.

My mother was as good as her word. The lawyer she had hired to take my case came to see me one evening. We met in the visiting room, at a table beyond the booths where I had talked with my mother. Here we could talk more freely. The lawyer sat down on one side of the table and I sat down on the other. No glass partition divided us.

My lawyer introduced himself. He was a distinguished-looking middle-aged man, very brisk and businesslike with glasses, three-piece suit, and briefcase. At first I didn't trust him. He intimidated me. As far as I could see, the questions he asked me had nothing to do with the crime. That made me uneasy.

"How many brothers and sisters do you have, Israel?"

"Eight," I answered slowly. "Six brothers and two sisters."

"I see," he said noncommittally, making a careful note of the information. "And how old are you?"

"Sixteen."

"Now, what kind of formal education have you had? Do you have your high school diploma?"

"Nope," I said, leaning back in my chair, my arms folded across my chest. I wondered what he was driving at.

"How far did you get in school, then?"

"Grade eight."

"Hmmmm. . . ."

"I started grade nine but I only went on and off," I volunteered.

"You played a lot of hooky, then, I gather?"

"Yeah. School didn't interest me very much."

"I see. . . ." He examined the notes in front of

him, and then asked me more of these trivial questions.

"But what does all this have to do with my case?" I asked him finally, in exasperation.

"Perhaps a great deal, and then again, perhaps nothing at all," he said evasively. "I like to probe into the background of all my clients—it gives me a greater appreciation and understanding of the kind of individual I'm representing. But have no fear, Israel. If you would prefer, we'll go on now to your involvement in the crime."

"Yeah."

"All right. Who was with you on the night of February 23?"

"Four guys . . . Chino, Melvin, Carlos, and Maximo—all MauMaus."

"Who was the one who actually fired the gun?"

"Chino."

"Did you have a weapon?"

"Yeah—a hunting knife. But I ditched it before the cops got us."

"I see. Did you use it?"

"Nah."

He referred to the notes in front of him. "Now why did you seek out this boy?"

"For revenge. He beat up one of our boys, so we had to get even."

"I see," his calm voice never registered surprise. "So you shot him?"

"We were jitter-bugging," I shrugged. "That's part of the game."

"Did you plan beforehand to kill him? In other words, did you intend to kill him?"

"That would be hard to say," I said sullenly.

"Now, Israel," he explained to me patiently. "This is extremely important. Look, I'm your lawyer—I'm on your side. I'm trying to help you, but I can't help you unless you answer all of my questions. You've got to trust me." He was very mild mannered; he never raised his voice at me once.

I shrugged. I wasn't in a very good bargaining position. He understood how the court of law worked—I didn't. I had no other choice but to tell him everything that he wanted to know.

"Now, did you plan to murder this boy? Was it premeditated?"

"Well, we were out to get him—mess him up. We had the gun, so there was a good chance that somebody was gonna get shot. But whether or not we were really gonna kill him—I don't know. These things are never planned." I shrugged. "They just happen. . . ."

The lawyer questioned me in detail about the night of the crime. I was bored with it all. Finally, he got up to go.

"Now, Israel," he told me, "I want you to be good while you're here. Stay out of trouble. Your behavior at this detention home is going to play an important part in your trial."

"OK, man," I nodded. "Look, how bad is it? How much time are we talking about?"

"Well, to be honest with you," he said cautiously, "you're facing twenty years."

I looked away. Twenty years! That was a real blow; I hadn't been expecting that much. As a lawyer he should know what he was talking about.

"But, we'll see what we can do. . . ." He shook my hand and gathered his papers, slipping them neatly into his briefcase. "Good night."

"Catch you later," I said absently, still thinking about what he had just told me. Twenty years. How would I be able to stand it?

"Well, man, you'll just have to take it as it comes . . ." I told myself philosophically.

The next day at lunch, Chino was in a black mood.

"Hey, whatsamatter?" Mel asked him jokingly. "The bedbugs bite you or something?"

"Aw, shut up," Chino snapped back.

"C'mon, man. What's eatin' you?" Carlos prodded. This wasn't like Chino at all.

"It's my brother," Chino scowled. "They jumped him, those dirty sons of—." He swore.

"Hey, man, what you talking about?" I asked him, perplexed.

"My old lady came to see me last night—" he said, pushing away his bowl of cornflakes. He had lost his appetite.

"So?" I urged him on.

"And she told me how those filthy Wops got my brother. Messed him up real bad!" Chino hissed through his teeth. He had only one brother, a kid of twelve years old, who resembled him very much.

"What Wops?" I asked quickly. "The Sand Street Angels?"

"Yeah, who else!" Chino snarled. "My old lady says there were three of them. . . ."

"Hey, guys, this is serious stuff," I told the

others, realizing the implications of the Angels'
actions. "All of our families are in danger. . . ."
Chino's brother may have been the first to be
badly beaten up, but not the last. I was worried
for my brothers. The Angels could attack them
any day on their way to or from school.

"Yeah," Carlos growled in agreement. "Those
jerks are out for revenge. . . ."

"Man, if I could only get my hands on those
creeps, I would tear them from limb to limb,"
Chino vowed angrily. I had never seen him so
worked up about anything before—he was usually so calm and reserved. He rammed his fist
down on the table, almost knocking over my tin
cup of milk. "But here I am stuck in this dunghole, and there's nothing I can do. . . ."

Filial loyalty stirred within all of us. We sat at
the lunch table, enraged with the Angels' actions
and our own impotence. But as Chino had stated, there was absolutely nothing we could do
about it—or so we thought.

A few days later, due to an amazing coincidence, Chino was given his chance. It happened
this way, while we were seated at our usual
table, engrossed in our evening meal.

"You seen a lawyer yet?" I asked Chino casually.

"Nah, not yet. . . ." He poked at his mashed
potatoes with his fork. "My old lady's trying
to—hey!" Chino stopped in midsentence, suddenly distracted. His eyes, narrowed to a slit,
were transfixed on something behind me. Turning around, I looked where he was looking.
There, hesitating just inside the door to the Day

Room, balancing his food tray and scanning the tables uncertainly for a place to sit down, was, unbelievably, an Angel. I recognized him as one of the Angels whom we had confronted at the Amusement Palace, and no doubt he was also one of the three who had jumped Chino's kid brother. By remarkable coincidence, he had been arrested, brought to the Atlantic Detention Home, and assigned to our floor!

Chino leaped to his feet and strode purposefully across the Day Room. Before the surprised Angel realized what was happening, Chino had grabbed him by the shirt collar and smashed him in the face. He fell backward, his tray clattering to the floor, splattering the walls with a mixture of mashed potato, spaghetti, and milk. Chino lunged on top of him and punched him again and again in the stomach, releasing the pent-up frustration of the last few days.

Seconds later the guard, who had been stationed outside of the Day Room, rushed over to break up the fight, wielding his billy-club. He grabbed Chino by the neck, yanking him away from the Angel. The Italian boy got to his feet slowly, clutching his stomach and swaying dizzily.

"I'm gonna kill you!" Chino hissed.

The Angel, still in shock, felt his bruised jaw and said nothing.

"All right. That's enough," the guard moved between the two boys, holding Chino back. He pushed them roughly out of the Day Room door.

"Man, Chino sure got him good," Mel whistled in appreciation, turning back to us.

"Yeah," I snickered. "That Angel didn't know what hit him!"

We didn't see Chino for the next three days and we sorely missed his presence at the meal table. For punishment, he was kept locked up in his cell, but we knew that the compensation of getting even far outweighed any discomfort he might feel. We never saw the Angel again. The guards thought it would be wise to move him to another floor.

My lawyer had warned me to stay out of trouble, but that was more easily said than done. We had been at the detention home for little more than a month when I found myself involved in a gang rumble.

From the beginning, we had noticed that most of the major gangs in Brooklyn had representatives on our floor: we had recognized members of the Viceroys, Chaplains, Dragons, Demons, and many others. So far we had had nothing to do with them; we had stayed out of each other's way, avoiding an outright confrontation. But we all knew, that with so many longstanding enemies grouped together on one floor, nursing bitter grudges, it was only a matter of time before volatile tempers were bound to ignite. Tonight was the night. I could almost feel a rumble coming.

Five members of the Comanches, a Negro gang, were sitting at the table directly in front of us. They were bragging loudly about how tough they were. Although we had never fought them, we knew that their reputation did not inspire the same degree of fear that ours did. We ate our meal in silence, listening to their vain boasting and growing angrier by the minute. We exchanged meaningful glances: we had had enough.

"Hey, man, cool it!" Carlos called over to their table. The five Comanches stopped talking abruptly and stared at us, astonished.

"Well, dig that dude . . ." the short fat one spluttered. "Man, just who do you think you're talking to? Nobody tells a Comanche to cool it!"

"Oh, yeah?" I sneered in contempt. "We do."

"And who are you?" another Comanche asked mockingly.

"Man, we're The People," Mel boasted. "We're the MauMaus."

"You look like the Chickens to me!" the gangly one at the end of the table snorted.

Another jeered, "You better not mess around with us—if you know what's good for you." He slapped his knee and guffawed.

"Yeah?" I challenged him, not raising my voice. "Why's that?"

"Cause we're the baddest dudes in New York City," he drawled.

Carlos sniffed. "We'll soon see about that."

"Man, we don't care about nobody!" the short one added.

"Well, we're the same way," Mel snarled, half rising to his feet.

"Then hey, man, let's get it on!" one of the Comanches cried, leaping to his feet.

A wild free-for-all broke out. We punched away at each other furiously. The guard on duty at the front door to the Day Room sounded the alarm, and a few minutes later the special riot squad stormed into the room, whistles shrieking and billy-clubs swinging. They charged right into the middle of the melee, grabbing us roughly by the shirt collars and tearing us apart. Then they dragged us outside into the open area and shoved our heads under the taps of the slop sinks along the wall, holding our heads under the cold water until all the fight in us had died.

Dripping, our shirts thoroughly soaked, we were taken back to our cells and locked up for the night. Furious, I ripped off my clammy shirt and undershirt and changed into another. After towel-drying my face and hair, I squeezed the water from my shirts and hung them on the bars to dry.

We were confined to our cells until the following evening when we were escorted to the "discipline court" one at a time. In this office, the Danish lieutenant questioned me:

"What caused the fight? How did it begin?"

I shrugged, rolling my eyeballs, "I dunno." I wasn't going to tell him what the fight had been about; that was none of his business.

"C'mon, Narvaez," he snapped. "You've got to know."

"Well, we just had a gang fight," I told him. "That's all. Nobody knows why it started. It just happened. . . ."

The lieutenant didn't take that answer very well. "Ah, you're all a bunch of no-goods. Every one of you—you're all the same," he said angrily. "Next time, it's not going to be so easy—I'm not going to be so lenient on you," he warned us.

"You guys could have got killed—you were enticing a riot! And that carries a penalty of two to three years if you go before a judge."

For punishment, I was confined to my cell for the next few days. All my meals were brought to me and I ate them sitting on my bed. Throughout the day, I paced back and forth across my cell. It took me two steps to get from one end to the other. One, two. Turn. One, two. Turn. Occasionally I stopped by the bars and, extending my arms through the spaces, I leaned my elbows on the crossbars and clasped my wrist on the outside. The sound of car horns and brakes carried up to my cell from the street below. I wondered when I was ever going to be able to walk down a street again. The streets were my real home.

"Man, I could sure use a bottle of wine right now," I thought to myself dismally. "And some grass. . . ."

EIGHT
"I Want to Live!"

"Hey, man, did you hear about Igor?" Little Man of the Viceroys slid onto the bench across the table from his pal Wyatt Earp.

Immediately Chino, Melvin, Carlos, and I perked up and turned our full attention toward the two Viceroys huddled at the end of our table. The fate of Igor was very important to the four of us. Indeed, our very lives were at stake. Igor was a husky eighteen-year-old Negro youth from the Bronx who had shot and killed a policeman. For the last month, everyone had been acutely aware of his approaching trial, and now that it was actually underway, there had been no other topic of conversation at the meal tables.

"No," Wyatt Earp shook his head in answer to Little Man's question. "Why? What's up?"

"He's gone, man!"

"To Sing-Sing?" Wyatt Earp asked slowly, expressing all of our fears.

"Yup," Little Man sighed, and then said pointedly, "and you know what that means . . . he got it."

We all knew what that meant: Igor had been sentenced to the electric chair.

Carlos was the first to come out of shock. He jumped up angrily. "Man, how do you know that?" he demanded of Little Man fiercely, unwilling to believe what he had just heard.

"Because," Little Man drawled, turning on his seat to face us, "Igor didn't come back from court today, that's why. Everybody else came back in the paddy wagon as usual—but not Igor. He was taken directly to Sing-Sing . . ."

"Baby, that's bad news." Mel jerked his head from side to side in nervous agitation.

Chino was hit hardest by the information. He pressed his palm to his forehead, pushed his food away in revulsion, and said nothing. I had never seen him so depressed.

"Man, what's gonna happen to us?" Carlos was brave enough to ask what all of us were privately thinking. "Are we gonna get the electric chair too?"

No one dared to answer him. In truth, we had all reached the same depressing conclusion: If Igor had received the death penalty for the murder of a policeman, then the four of us, who had committed a like crime, could also receive the same sentence.

"Man, I don't want to be fried like no egg," I exploded in anguish. I had seen some grisly movies about people dying in the electric chair. For one horror-filled moment, I imagined myself strapped to a chair with a helmet connected to wires on my head. I saw the executioner pull the switch. I heard the crackling of electrical current and smelled the sizzling of human flesh, my flesh . . .

"No way, man!" Chino burst out. "Me neither!"

"We may have no choice in the matter!" Carlos remarked sarcastically.

"But I'm too young to die," Mel groaned, feverishly rocking back and forth on the bench.

"Yeah, man, they can't do that to us," I rebelled. "Zap. Goodbye. Game over." It was bad enough that "they" had taken our freedom away from us, but to know that they had the power to take away our life was outrageous.

"Wanna make a bet?" Carlos snorted. "They can do whatever they want to us."

We lapsed into an agonized silence, all preoccupied with our own morbid thoughts. It was hard to accept the fact that other people had complete power over our destinies, that they had the undisputed authority to actually end our lives! In a few seconds, they could pull the switch and our lives would be snuffed out for all eternity! We were utterly dependent on the mercy of the court. Our lives rested in its hands.

Of course, now I know that no man has authority over our lives, except as God allows him. And we were not dependent on the mercy of the earthly court, but on the mercy of our Eternal Judge.

The day that we heard of Igor's sentence

marked a turning point in all of our lives. From that day on, our whole attitude radically changed. For the past five months, we had joked about our crime and our approaching trial. But now everything was suddenly different. The four of us became very solemn and morose, withdrawn and introspective.

For the first time in my life, I considered what it would mean to die. I had never given the important subject much thought before. Indeed, I had been too busy fighting and killing others. Seeing other boys dying had not bothered me. When I had seen the Angel shot and killed, it meant nothing to me. Somehow, when it was your own life at stake, however, it was another matter entirely!

Sometimes before going into a rumble, the thought had crossed my mind fleetingly that maybe today it would be my turn to die. But always, I had pushed it back stubbornly, refusing to face the possibility of my own death. If I had let myself honestly acknowledge that possibility, fear would have overcome me and I would have showed signs of cowardice, something no respectable gang leader was allowed to do. So a long time ago, I had willfully blocked off this frightening avenue of thought.

"I'm not ready to die," I moaned to myself at night, while tossing and turning on my cot. "I want to live!"

The more I contemplated death, the more I appreciated life. Life gained a whole new meaning, a fresh significance for me. For the first time, I began to value human life—any life—but

especially *my own*. I thought of all the things I
wanted to do and hadn't done yet. I thought of
all my secret ambitions and hopes and dreams
that would now never be realized. Like becoming
a rock 'n roll star or a movie actor like Hum-
phrey Bogart or James Cagney—I had always
dreamed of becoming a *somebody!* But now, before I had a chance to accomplish any of these
things, my life was about to be snuffed out.

Every moment became precious to me. For the
past five months I had found the monotonous
daily routine of the Atlantic Detention Home
boring. The endless waiting had been the worst
part—not knowing how long I was going to have
to stay there, not knowing what was going to
happen to me or when it was going to happen.
The confinement to a cell for most of the day
and night had made me afraid that I might go
crazy. I hadn't known what to do with myself.
To kill time, I had played silly games with
myself. Sometimes I had thrown my pillow up
into the air and punched it, or I had propped it
against the wall and beaten it with my fists.
Sometimes I had molded wet bits of toilet paper
into small blobs and tossed them through the
bars onto the floor below, or aimed them at an
imaginary target on the wall opposite my bed,
where they had stuck like glue. It had been
harmless fun, but when the guards caught me in
the act, they ordered me to stop.

At other times, I had sat on my cot with my
back against the wall and listened by earphone to
all the latest hits on the radio. My favorite songs
were love songs: "The Great Pretender" and

"The Magic Touch" by the Platters and "It's Not for Me to Say" by Johnny Mathis. If the song had a good beat, I snapped my fingers to the rhythm, and if I really got carried away, I sang the song out loud. A lot of the other boys in the cell block had been crooning along to their favorites at the same time, but occasionally one of my grumpier neighbors would complain.

Now, however, instead of finding the detention home routine excruciatingly boring, I enjoyed it. Instead of just trying to kill time, I tried to make each passing moment count. I clung to each one as if it were my last. Every little action had become just that important, an affirmation of life. Now when I went upstairs to the gym, I participated with enthusiasm and vigor in *all* the activities. I appreciated just being alive—feeling my lungs expand and my muscles tighten. The minutes didn't drag anymore—they passed all too quickly!

One day, while sitting in my cell, I noticed that the floor needed cleaning. I decided to do something constructive. I got down on my hands and knees and started scrubbing the floor with my extra toothbrush—the only available tool I had—and a bar of soap and water. Painstakingly, I scrubbed it inch by inch. After a few days, the bristles of my toothbrush were worn out, but the dirty concrete floor was beginning to turn a shiny white.

One of the guards, Mr. Seeley, noticed my industrious activity one morning as he passed my cell. He paused on the catwalk and watched me.

"You're doing a fine job, there," he commented. "The floor looks pretty good."

"Thanks," I nodded absently and went on scrubbing, absorbed in my project. Mr. Seeley was an OK guard. He never tried to push me around or get on my back as some of the other guards did. He treated all of the inmates like men, not animals.

"You like to keep things clean, huh?" he remarked conversationally.

"Yup." My mother had brought me up that way.

"How would you like to work in the kitchen?" he asked me. I was surprised by the suggestion.

"Sure," I shrugged, not wanting to show how delighted I was with the idea. "Why not?" I knew that the kitchen staff got out of their cells ahead of the other inmates and returned to their cells after everybody else. The longer I could stay out of that hole, the happier I was—that was the name of the whole game.

"OK," Mr. Seeley smiled, "I'll arrange it so that you can work in the kitchen." He winked, "We need clean people down there."

And so I was put on trial duty in the kitchen. Twenty minutes before every meal, I would slip a white full-length apron over my head and then wheel the catering wagons off the elevators over to their appropriate places in the open area between the cell blocks. Next I would stack the trays and arrange the pots of food and get everything ready. When the inmates lined up in front of the catering wagons, I and three others would spoon out portions of food onto their trays.

Sometimes Chino, Mel, and Carlos would come by in my lineup and I would say, "Hi, guys. What's happening?" They would reply with a smart remark and we would exchange wisecracks. Sometimes I would scoop out a generous portion of food and splat it down on their trays sloppily.

"Hey, man," Chino would feign anger. "Watch what you're doin'."

One of the disadvantages to the job was that I couldn't eat with Chino, Mel, and Carlos anymore. The kitchen workers had to wait until everybody else was taken back to their cells before we could eat. Then we could eat whatever was left over—as much as we wanted. I would sit with the other three workers at the nearest table and we would pick at our food slowly, trying to stay out of our cells as long as possible. My fellow workers changed constantly. Usually they were in on lesser charges such as car theft, possession of marijuana or dangerous weapons. Although our floor was for homicide, most of the time quite a few cells were empty so the overflow from other floors was brought to our floor. As their trials came up, my co-workers were replaced.

After we finished our meal, we would wash down the tables in the Day Room, fold and push them to one side, and sweep the floor. We would stack all the trays and leftover food back onto the catering wagons and then wheel them back onto the elevators and return to our cells. We would work as slowly as possible, but the guards didn't mind.

The thought of the electric chair constantly haunted me. When my mother came for her visits, as she faithfully did almost every evening, she sensed that something was bothering me.

"Is anything wrong, Israel?" she asked me suspiciously.

"Nah, everything's OK," I hastily reassured her. "There's nothing to worry about—I didn't kill anybody, so don't worry. . . ."

But inside I was asking myself, "How's she gonna feel when she finds out I'm going to the electric chair?" and then, "It'll break her—" I never brought up this subject with her. I never discussed my innermost fears with anybody—not even Chino, Mel, or Carlos.

"Anna came over to the apartment last night," my mother informed me casually.

I looked up. Anna was the girl I had been going with before I got arrested. "Yeah?" I replied, trying to sound disinterested. "What did she have to say?"

"She says she's gonna wait for you . . ." my mother half smiled. "She must really like you, Israel."

"Nah," I brushed it off, embarrassed, then frowned. "Well, you better tell her not to wait." Then I added bitterly, "She'd be wasting her life. I'm gonna be in here a long time." If not six-feet-under pretty soon, I thought to myself.

"You should see a priest, Israel," my mother urged me for the hundredth time. "You're always promising me that you'll go and see a priest. Have you gone yet?"

"Nah. . . ."

"Israel," my mother pouted in disappointment.

"Aw, Mom. I'll get around to it one of these days. . . ."

"Promise me that you'll go to mass—or confession at least," she pleaded, fingering the cross around her neck.

"Yeah," I shrugged. Of course, I had no intention of either going to a priest, mass, or confession. Even with my Catholic upbringing, I wasn't thinking about heaven or hell or judgment or punishment or life after death. Even in my deepest fear, I refused to turn to God. "I'll go next Sunday . . ." I lied.

The next day, the guard brought a priest to my cell. He was an elderly man with a kindly face, decked out in his collar and robes.

"Your mother wanted me to speak with you—so here I am," he said.

I grunted. He seemed like an OK guy. He also said he would speak for me in court, and then, "I would like to pray for you, Israel. Will you pray with me?"

As he rambled on, I looked at the floor sheepishly and waited for him to finish. "Prayer doesn't do anything," I told myself cynically. "And no priest can help me!"

Prison bars can't block the Spirit of the Lord—only the bars of the human heart can delay his work.

My seventeenth birthday passed by unheralded in June. I had been locked up for six months now. Vaguely I wondered if this birthday would be my last. . . .

Nightmares about going to the electric chair constantly tormented me. In my mind, I would be terrified by a giant switch slowly being pulled down—the one that controlled the thousand volts—and I would wake up in a cold sweat. The thought of the electric chair was always before me. How could I block it out of my mind?

As the trial date edged nearer, the four of us were getting more uptight and tense with each passing moment. The trial was always on the tip of our tongues. We discussed our situation, weighing the alternatives.

"Man, how should we plead?" Carlos asked. "Guilty or innocent?"

"I don't care," Mel shrugged. He seemed the least affected by the whole affair. "Can't you guys ever talk about anything else? That's all we talk about anymore and I'm sick of it!"

"Look, Melvin," I told him. "It's important. Don't you care whether you live or die?"

Mel shrugged. "Baby, if I die, I die. There ain't much I can do about it one way or the other."

"Everybody says that if you plead guilty, you get off easier," I said. "Everybody" was the boys who had been through the whole court procedure before—the guys who were in the "know." They had spread the word along to us.

"Yeah, that's right," Chino agreed. "It's called plea bargaining."

"I think that's what we should do," I said emphatically. "If we plead guilty, we won't risk getting the electric chair. . . ." All that mattered to me now was my life. I didn't care whether I had to spend the next twenty years of my life in jail, I just didn't want to die. Anything was better than that. Anything!

"Cool," Carlos also agreed with my decision. "Sounds good to me."

Later we discussed our plea of guilty with our lawyers and they agreed that it was the best thing we could do. I respected their judgment. They were going to try to arrange an under-the-table plea bargain with the judge. Melvin, Carlos, and I were going to plead guilty to the charge of manslaughter in the first degree and Chino was going to plead guilty to the charge of murder in the second degree.

The four of us became very anxious to go to court and get the whole thing over with. The suspense about our eventual sentence was eating away at us. As far as I was concerned, our day in court couldn't come soon enough!

NINE
The Big Day

Of how much sorer punishment, suppose
ye, shall he be thought worthy, who hath
trodden under foot the Son of God, and
hath counted the blood of the covenant,
wherewith he was sanctified, an unholy
thing, and hath done despite unto the Spirit
of grace? (Hebrews 10:29).

Immediately after breakfast on that January
morning of 1960, Chino, Mel, Carlos, and I were
assembled together, handcuffed, and locked in
the back of a paddy wagon.

"Well, guys," Chino said nervously. "This is
it. Today's the *big day*."

"Yeah, man," I sighed, "I'm glad it's going to
be all over soon." After being locked up for
almost a year in the Atlantic Detention Home,
the day of our sentencing had finally arrived.

"Whadya think we're gonna get?" Carlos asked

the million-dollar question for the thousandth time. "Five to fifteen? Ten to twenty? Any bets?"

We were all trying to put on a brave front, but inside we were quaking. Our future would be decided today. We joked to cover our nervousness, exchanging banter about our court appearance and its probable outcome, but the conversation soon took on a more serious note. We became very solemn and treated the occasion with the respect it deserved.

When we reached the courthouse, a guard unlocked the back doors of the paddy wagon, swinging them wide open, and we all piled out, jumping to the pavement awkwardly. As I walked up the steps to the court buildings, I looked around me, wide eyed, taking a deep breath of the frosty air—it seemed ages since I had been outside.

"Man, I'd give anything to walk down that street a free man," I sighed. How many years would pass before I would be able to do something as simple and taken-for-granted as that?

Inside the courthouse, the four of us were kept locked up in the holding tank until the scheduled time of our sentencing. Finally our turn came.

As we entered the crowded courtroom, everyone turned to stare at us. I concentrated on the hairy nape of Mel's neck as he walked in front of me, but suddenly, out of the blur of faces, I caught sight of the huddled form of my mother. She was propped up against my aunt, her sister, who had probably come along to give her much-needed moral support. As we approached their bench, the second from the front, my mother turned to look at me, but I avoided her glance and kept staring straight ahead. Somehow, I just couldn't bring myself to meet her eyes.

We sat down in our reserved benches at the front of the courtroom, surrounded by our lawyers and their assistants and district attorneys. The four of us were strangely quiet and serious. We kept very still, hardly moving, as if we were carved in stone. When the judge entered the courtroom, everyone rose respectfully and the official procedure of the court got underway. The judge called us forward to stand in front of him as he read out the formal charges against us— manslaughter in the first degree. He asked us how we pleaded.

"Guilty, your honor," I mumbled quietly when my turn came.

Next the lawyers were given a last opportunity to present the extenuating circumstances of our case. Each of our lawyers gave an eloquent speech about the four of us being "victims of our environment" and other fancy-phrased nonsense. I thought my lawyer delivered a good speech. I didn't believe all that he said, but it sounded good anyway, and that's what he was getting paid for.

"He's a good mouthpiece," I grunted to myself in approval. I was only half listening to him; my mind was preoccupied. The whole time I kept my eyes on the judge's lined face, watching it closely for any reaction.

"How many years will he give us?" I asked myself over and over again. The question hammered its way through all my thoughts. "How many years? How many years?" By now, I had worked myself into a very tense state of emotion: I was on edge, nervous, uneasy. I shifted my weight back from one foot to the other and kept my hands clenched tightly behind my back. The suspense was killing me.

The prison priest was called forward to speak in our behalf. In a brief statement, he explained to the judge that he had counseled us at the detention home and that he thought we were basically good but mixed-up kids. I watched the judge's face, but when he turned abruptly to look back at me, I squirmed uncomfortably. He had very penetrating eyes—eyes that missed nothing.

"He looks like he can see right through me," I muttered to myself uneasily. "We're not fooling him one little bit."

At last the judge called the four of us forward again.

"Well, Israel baby," I said to myself, swallowing hard, "this is it." I hoped that the judge would be lenient with us.

The next few moments were the longest moments of my life. I hardly breathed as the judge read out the sentence he was giving to us. He addressed himself to Carlos, Mel, and me first. I listened intently to every word he said, keenly, painfully, expectantly. But hard as I tried, I couldn't understand all the legal mumble-jumble. When the judge finished passing sentence on us, I was as much in the dark as ever. Mel, Carlos, and I exchanged troubled glances. They were as confused as I was.

"Man, I still don't know how many years I'm gonna get," I complained to myself in frustration. It sounded like the judge had given us an indefinite sentence. I was really scared now.

After barely pausing to catch his breath, the judge continued his monologue, this time addressing himself solely to Chino. And what he said to Chino was clear to everybody: because of the nature of the crime and the circumstances involved, he was forced to give Chino the maximum penalty—twenty years to life.

I was looking at Chino as the judge uttered these words. They hit him like a physical blow. He bowed his head and closed his eyes and one hand gripped the wrist of the other, his fingernails digging into his flesh: he was a broken young man. I knew that he had been expecting something in the range of ten to twenty years, but not this—not life! He was crushed.

As the judge finished speaking, I heard my mother crying two rows behind me. I turned around to look at her, and it was only then that I noticed the tall, lanky figure beside her—my father. My mother didn't look up at me. She was bent over, her face buried in a handkerchief. My father put his arm around her shoulder and vainly tried to comfort her. Over her head, my father glared at me accusingly, as if to say: "You must be crazy!" I had never seen him looking so dark and fierce before.

I turned away quickly. It hurt me to see my mother so badly shaken.

We were escorted back to the holding tank downstairs. The three of us didn't speak to

Chino, at least not directly. We had nothing to say to him. No jokes. No words of hope. Nothing. What could we say to a seventeen-year-old kid who was facing life imprisonment? What could anyone say?

I had never seen Chino so shattered before. He stood all alone in the far corner of the cell, his arms crossed tightly against his chest as if he were holding himself, wrapped in his own thoughts. I doubt if he was even conscious of us—he was far, far away.

Carlos, Mel, and I huddled together at the front of the cell, discussing our sentence in hushed tones.

"Hey, guys, how much time did we get?" I asked them.

They were as baffled as I was.

"Don't ask me." Mel rolled his eyeballs. "I didn't understand nothin'!"

"Me neither," Carlos shrugged. "All I heard was something about an indefinite sentence."

"And that don't sound too good," I muttered, cracking my knuckles nervously.

A few minutes later, our lawyers came into our cells, all smiles.

"What's there to smile about?" I growled to myself irritably.

Our lawyers took each of us aside and spoke to us individually.

"Well, what's the news?" I asked my lawyer. "What's happening, man?"

"The maximum time you'll have to serve is five years—" my lawyer began.

"Five years!" I shouted, relieved to know

the worst. Five years wasn't too bad, considering. . . .

"And," he continued almost merrily, "the eleven months that you spent in the detention home count toward your sentence. So in actual fact, the absolute maximum time that you have left to serve is only four years. . . ." The way he put it, it sounded like a lucky break.

"And not only that," my lawyer grinned, "if you behave yourself, you could be out on parole in two years."

I sighed deeply, immensely relieved. After expecting the death penalty, and then hearing Chino's sentence of twenty years to life, four years seemed like a very short time indeed. Of course, I was going to find out that four years in prison was still a great deal of time; but for the moment, I was optimistic.

"Good luck." My lawyer shook my hand, obviously anxious to leave. He had performed his duty. "Good luck and goodbye."

And that was it—for a thousand bucks. I never saw him again.

On the way back to the Atlantic Detention Home, Carlos, Melvin, and I talked back and forth excitedly. After so many months of worry, the future didn't look so black after all.

"It's not too bad," Carlos said, referring to our sentence.

I nodded. "We'll probably be turned loose in a couple of years!"

"Crazy, baby," Mel exclaimed, his eyes dancing in his head.

We stopped talking, suddenly acutely conscious of Chino. He sat with his back against the side panel, sullen and grim. Up until now, the four of us had been all together in the same boat, but now we were separated—three and one. We couldn't share Chino's burden. It was his to bear and his alone. Our unequal sentencing had placed a barrier between us. Chino was naturally envious of us. When we tried to cheer him up, he ignored us. From the sour expression on his face, he was probably thinking, "Yeah, you guys can talk, you lucky son-of-a-guns! You've only got four years and I've got twenty to life!"

We didn't blame him for questioning the justice of the sentencing. But whether it was fair or not, the three of us were glad for the sentence we had received. We felt sorry for Chino, but there was nothing we could do about it. . . .

That evening, my mother came to visit me. My father didn't show up.

"Oh, Israel," she sobbed, tears streaming down her cheeks. "What will you do?" My mother's nerves were shot; she was strained to the breaking point.

"Don't worry, Mom," I shrugged. "I'll be OK. I'll manage."

"But it's such a long time . . ." she moaned.

"Nah. It's only four years at the most. Maybe two if I get out on parole," I said, trying to comfort her. "That's not too bad. It could be a whole lot worse."

But my mother wasn't comforted by that information at all. I watched helplessly as she sat in the booth across from me, crying and shaking her head and rocking back and forth, lost in a mother's deep grief and anguish.

"Do you know where they're sending you?" she managed to choke out the words.

"Elmira. It's in upstate New York," I said.

"Ohhh, such a long way away," my mother sighed. "Well, I'll visit you as often as I can. I don't know where I'm going to get money for the train fare," she fussed, "but don't worry, I'll do my best."

And then we parted. "Be good, son. Stay out of trouble."

"Yeah, Mom. Sure," I said, hiding my emotion. "Catch you later."

When would I see her again?

TEN
Bitter Hours

"Hey, look at that nice-lookin' old lady out there," I said to Mel, jerking my chin in the direction of the young girl about to board the next passenger car down from ours. I wasn't able to point with my finger because my left wrist was handcuffed to Melvin's right, and my other was shackled to the thick leather belt around my waist. The two of us, along with eighteen other convicts, including Chino and Carlos, were being transferred by regular train in a reserved car to the Elmira Correctional Facility and Reception Center in upstate New York.

Mel whistled in appreciation, his eyes dancing in his head, "Yeah, baby, that mama's out of sight!"

"I wonder what kind of perfume she's wearing?" I mused sentimentally. It had been a long time—too long—since I had laid eyes on a delectable young female. How I yearned to hold a girl in my arms, to nuzzle my cheek against a soft neck. . . .

"But who cares about the perfume," I continued, "as long as she's a girl!"

"There's gonna be a lot of 'girls' where we're goin' now," Mel reminded me with a touch of black humor.

"Yeah," I responded drily, "but they ain't the kind of girls I'm interested in."

"Maybe not. But they may be interested in *you!*" Mel teased me, trying to make me mad. "Man, with your smooth chin—they're all gonna be chasin' after you!"

"Aw, shut up," I growled irritably. I didn't think his crack was very funny—it was too close to the truth. The prison grapevine had warned us that homosexuals preferred younger boys with smooth, clean-shaven faces, and as I hadn't started to shave yet, I fit the bill. Perfectly. Mel, on the other hand, with his goatee and mustache and generally hairy face, could afford to tease me.

"Man, nobody's gonna turn me into a trick," I told Melvin fervently. "I'm prepared to do anything! If I have to fight, I'll fight. If I gotta stab somebody, I'll stab. Simple as that. Nothing's gonna stop me!" I vowed earnestly.

"Yeah, I'm with you all the way," Mel agreed solemnly. "If I gotta turn somebody on, baby, I'm gonna do it. Nobody's gonna turn me into a trick!"

We lapsed into silence. I stared out the window at the snowcovered Catskill Mountains. After eleven months of being cooped up in a ten-by-six cage, it gave me a good feeling to gaze at the wide open outdoors——an all-too-brief glimpse of freedom. I wasn't really paying much attention to the passing scenery, however, because I was thinking about my prison term. I was psyching myself up to face the coming ordeal.

"Four years behind bars," I muttered to myself miserably. "Four long years. Man, I'm goin' up the river now. . . ."

I tried to decide the attitude and behavior that I would adopt at Elmira. I knew that I had two choices of how I could "do" my time: I could let the days slide by and make myself as invisible as possible, or I could act mean and make my presence felt. Certainly, I would have to be tough, and on occasion, fight to preserve my reputation. But on the other hand, I didn't want to go to extremes and be branded as a troublemaker. Well, I was going to do what I had to do. . . .

"OK, everybody up and out," the guard at the front of the car ordered us. The train had pulled into the sleepy town of Elmira and the guards had unlocked the chains that bound the foot of each convict sitting by the aisle to the foot of the convict behind him. Two by two (I was still handcuffed to Melvin) we shuffled awkwardly down the aisle and stepped onto the platform. The other people congregated on the platform, who were waiting to board the train, shied away from us as if we were contaminated. I felt like some kind of tamed beast, a circus bear—subhuman.

As I waited passively for the guards to order us to move, a strange thing happened to me; I was transported back in time. Across my mind flashed a vivid image of that day over a year and a half ago when I had stood on this very same platform. But then, instead of being among a group of convicts bound for prison, I had been with Rev. Wilkerson and my fellow ex-MauMau Nicky, on my way to give my testimony in a large tent meeting in the town of Elmira that night. Everything had been radically different then: the trip had been an exciting adventure, I had been happy in my newfound faith, and Jesus had been very real to me.

As the three of us had stood waiting for our ride, a group of sixteen convicts, chained and handcuffed as I myself now was, had stepped off the train. As they had approached us, I had recognized some of them as Hellburners, a brother gang from Brooklyn.

"Hey, what's happening, man?" I had asked as I walked over to them. "What you get busted for?"

Before they had time to answer, one of the guards had blocked my path. "Hey, you can't talk to the prisoners," he had informed me. "Stand back."

I had obeyed, but not before I had shouted over my shoulder, "See you later!"

Now, with a shock, I realized just how prophetic those words of mine had been. As I had watched them tramp away, I never imagined that I myself would be in their exact position, in the same unfortunate circumstances, only a year and a half later. At that time I had stood on the threshold of a whole new life; prison indeed had seemed like a remote possibility for my future.

"And look at me now," I shook my head bitterly, trying to brush away memories I couldn't cope with. "That creep preacher. If I hadn't been left deserted on a street corner—"

"Get a move on," a guard's booming voice brought me sharply back to the present. We were herded onto a bus and driven to the reformatory on the outskirts of the town. As we approached the high twenty-foot walls, guarded by watch-towers on all corners, I was reminded of the old Fort Greene prison in the center of the park. From the steps of the monument, I had often looked down into the exercise yard below where a guard with a rifle had watched the inmates from his tower. As the bus drove through the open gates, everyone was silent. We were entering an alien world. The outside world was firmly shut behind us.

"Well, this is it," I told myself as we were hustled into the thirty-floor building in front of us, which reminded me of a warehouse. "This is the moment of truth."

Fear was beginning to gnaw at my insides. Would I survive? Would I get out of this place alive? All the horrible rumors that I had heard about prison life assailed me at once—rumors of rape, beatings, and murder.

"Hold it, man," I scolded myself. "Take it easy. Just take everything as it comes. One step at a time." I got a grip on my runaway thoughts and mentally steeled myself for the worst. I knew that if I ever showed any sign of fear, if the other cons sensed it in me, my game would be over.

Inside a large room on the first level, the prison personnel asked us all the routine questions . . . name, birthdate, height, weight, place of birth, etc. We each stepped in turn behind a narrow board which had five numbers pasted on it, to have our mug shots taken. We had to memorize this identification number—it was used on our files, on our mail, and on our clothes when they were sent to the laundry. Next we were ordered to strip and were taken to the showers which were off to one side of the room. Then, wet and naked, all twenty of us were lined up in a row while two inmates, each carrying a large aluminum can, much like a milk can, sprayed us with a disinfectant—in case we had lice.

I tensed as the inmate sprayed me. Cautiously I watched him to make sure that he wasn't eyeing me lustfully—but he was just going about his business. Other inmates walked by, performing their regular duties and sometimes glancing in our direction. Our bodies were exposed to all curious eyes and I knew that that was a very dangerous thing in prison.

Finally a guard tossed us each a couple of pairs of dark blue denim jeans and workshirts, the regulation prison uniform, and we were escorted to the fourth floor, the area of the prison complex known as "reception." Chino, Mel, and Carlos were locked up in cells a few down from mine. From my own cell, I could look through a regular window down into a small courtyard below. Sometimes I saw a guard or an inmate walking across it.

For the next month we were isolated from the general prison population while we were screened. The authorities thoroughly examined us, giving us all sorts of psychological and I.Q. tests, in order to categorize us in terms of our attitude, intelligence, and behavior. Word quickly spread among us that if these tests showed that we could be rehabilitated, we would likely stay at Elmira, for Elmira had a reputation as a model prison and state showplace. If they did not, we would be shipped out elsewhere.

While we were being graded like eggs, the four of us passed the time by shouting back and forth to each other in our cells. Sometimes we discussed the tests that we had gone through that day to prepare the others in case they had to take the same ones the next day.

"Hey, man," Melvin called out one afternoon, "I went to see the shrink today. The guy's crazy! He asked me if I ever went to bed with my sister and all kinds of weird stuff like that. . . ."

Coming from Melvin, it wasn't hard to figure out why the psychiatrist had asked the questions he did. Melvin had to be the best case study that anybody could ask for!

During the last week of reception, it became common knowledge where they were sending us.

"Hey, where you goin'?" Chino asked Carlos one day at lunch.

Carlos smiled mischievously. "Wallkill."

"Wallkill! You lucky son-of-a-gun. They ain't

got no walls there!" Wallkill was a minimum security prison.

"That's right. . . ."

"Man, it's not fair," Chino scowled, clearly envious of Carlos. He thought he was getting a lucky break, getting off too easy.

"Well, where are you headed?" Carlos asked him in turn.

Chino snorted. "Great Meadows." Great Meadows was a maximum security prison for hardcore criminals. Nobody envied Chino. He wasn't very happy about his fate either.

"How about you, Mel?" I asked, breaking the awkward silence. "Where are they sending you?"

"Woodburn," he drawled in his usual slack-jawed way. Woodburn was the place they sent the mentally disturbed boys. "What about you?"

"Well, I don't have very far to go," I laughed. "For better or worse, I'm staying right here."

Melvin was the first of us to go. I was in my cell when he walked by for the last time.

"Catch you later, man," I called out to him, waving. He couldn't wave back because his hands were full. "Keep cool and don't get into any trouble."

"I won't," he shrugged. "Don't worry about it."

"Well, see you around," I called again desperately, as he disappeared from my line of vision and my life. I was never to see Melvin again.

"Yeah, we'll see you later, Mel. Take it easy," I could hear Chino and Carlos yelling in unison from further down the tier.

My turn to go came next. At 10 A.M. the

following day, a guard came for me without warning. I had no chance to say a final goodbye to Chino and Carlos—they were taking the last of their tests. Later I found out that according to the examinations, Carlos was a very intelligent young man, the most intelligent of us all. At Wallkill he was treated very well, and after serving only a year there, he was released. In society again, he smartened up and settled down, and when I chanced to meet him on a street in the Bronx six years later, he was very clean and respectable looking. Melvin, on the other hand, grew wilder. Shortly after he was released, somebody beat up his brother, and in revenge, Melvin stabbed and killed him. He was sent back to prison again for murder. And as for Chino— well, I was to meet up with him sooner than I had expected. . . .

One evening a "hack" came by and stopped in front of my cell. He wasn't one of the usual hacks who patrolled this cell block and I wondered what he wanted with me. Was I in some kind of trouble? At first he didn't say anything, he just looked at me with an odd expression on his face. Unnerved, I came over to the bars.

"Anything wrong, mister?" I wasn't one to pull any punches.

"Yeah, lots," he answered sourly. "What happened?"

I was taken aback. I didn't know what to say. "Man, I don't know what you're talking about," I said defensively. Who was this guy, anyway?

"Yes, you do," he said firmly, then added, "I

was there, you know. At the tent meeting Rev. Wilkerson held in the town. . . ."

I snorted. "So what?" I was angry now. As soon as he mentioned Wilkerson's name, bitterness washed over me like a cold tide. I never wanted to hear about that preacher or that tent meeting or anything to do with religion again. Why couldn't this man just go away and leave me alone?

The hack went on, oblivious to my scowl, "I heard you speak—"

"That's all over with now," I interrupted angrily.

"—and you know something?" the hack continued as if he hadn't heard me. "I really believed in you. I thought you had really changed and that something wonderful had come out of your life. . . ."

"Well, you were wrong, mister," I mocked him bitterly.

He paused and then continued, his voice thick with discouragement, " . . . and now here you are in this cell." He shook his head sadly.

"What's it to you?" I cried. Why should this man care what happened to me?

"I really thought there was hope . . ." he said more to himself than to me. His words held a note of defeat. His eyes looked accusing, as if he were blaming me for something.

"Yeah, well, that's the way life goes," I said drily, intending to end the conversation right then. It had gone far enough.

"What happened?" he asked. The conversation had come full circle.

"Look, man, I don't dig your questions," I said fiercely. "I don't want to talk about it." Why couldn't this hack just mind his own business and leave me in peace?

My words must have finally gotten through to him because he left abruptly. We saw each other around the compound after that, but always at a distance. We never spoke again. He seemed to want to avoid me as much as I wanted to avoid him.

Only years later did I remember this incident as God placed it upon my heart. I realize now that this guard had been touched in some way at that tent meeting. Perhaps his faith had been rekindled or he had accepted Christ as his Savior. At any rate, I played a part in his disillusionment, and for this I am sorry. When we fall, we don't know how many people we are letting down, how many people may be affected by our fall, how many people may stumble themselves because of it. No man is an island. Each of our lives affects other lives. When we stand before Christ, we shall be held responsible for our every word, thought, and action.

ELEVEN
Marching Orders

One of the things I hated most about life at Elmira was the marching. Every morning after breakfast all the prisoners, about twelve hundred men, were assembled in the courtyard and divided into companies of thirty. Then, in our winter Eisenhower air force jackets, we were forced to march around inside the large empty armory building, holding wooden rifles against our shoulders, just as if we were in the regular militia. Inmates were assigned positions of command over the companies and they drilled us, shouting orders of:

"Left. Right. Left. Halt!" or "About face!" or "Present arms!"

I loathed every minute of it—and we were required to march thirty minutes every day. I felt like one of the wooden soldiers I had played with as a kid. I didn't see the point in being drilled like a soldier if I was never going to become one. And I certainly wasn't planning on joining the army when I was released—the government had already taken five years of my life away and that was enough!

The purpose of the marching was of course to promote discipline among the population, but it failed miserably with me. If anything, it increased my rebellion against authority. When I marched, I marched as sloppily and lazily as I could. Sometimes the guards who were stationed around the building, inspecting the troops from the sidelines, would yell at me: "Hey you! Pick up your feet!" or "Hey there! Get into step!" (When everybody else was marching left-right-left, I was stubbornly marching right-left-right.)

I didn't pay any attention to the guards' orders. Instead, I filed by them, scowling insolently, becoming increasingly surly and uncooperative as the days passed by.

After the marching, I was forced to attend school classes for the morning. I had no choice in the matter. The prison authorities had set up a daily program for me and I was forced to follow it.

In the regular public school system I had made it to the eighth grade, but the prison authorities, after examining my I.Q. results, decided to make me repeat grade eight again. Actually, I don't know how I ever managed to pass the eighth grade in the first place, since by that time I had become heavily involved with the gangs, skipping most of my classes in favor of jitter-bugging.

Up until grade eight I had been an average student. I had got along fairly well with most of my teachers and, in fact, I had even been my homeroom teacher's pet. At lunch hours, I often ran to the store and bought fruit and yogurt for her. She had been very friendly to me and never raised her voice at me. But in the other classes it had been a different story: I was forever getting into trouble for disturbing the class. I had thrown paper clips and rubber bands at my fellow classmates and spitballs at the ceiling. When the teachers caught me, they made me stand in the corner for punishment.

Once when I hadn't been paying attention, my math teacher hit me on the head with a book. My immediate reaction was to swear at him, and for this I had been expelled. Before I was allowed to return to class, I had to bring my mother to the principal's office and then I had to apologize to my math teacher in front of everybody, which had been very humiliating—especially because I had a crush on two of the prettier girls in the class.

Even back then I hadn't liked school very much—most of the time I thought it was a waste of time. I would rather have been roaming the streets. I had had no career in mind and no particular goals in life. For grade nine, I had attended Metropolitan High School in Manhattan with some vague notion of becoming a merchant seaman—not because I had really wanted to, but because it had seemed to be the best of a poor range of choices. I had thought I would enjoy traveling and seeing more of the world than the ghettos of New York—I guess my merchant marine father had influenced me somewhat. The school had its own boat docked at the pier and at the few classes I had attended, I learned how to scrape and paint a boat and to cook. I soon lost interest in an education entirely; the gang had become my only obsession.

When I should have been in class, I was out riding the subways with the other gang members, terrorizing the passengers, stealing hats off old men, and then jumping out the doors before they realized what had happened. Or we had stood on the platform and, just before the subway doors closed, we sprayed a stinking mixture of flour and water onto the well-groomed heads of the businessmen sitting near the doors. As the train had gathered speed, we had run along beside it, waving at the furious victims.

On hot days, we had gone swimming in the East River, jumping off the piers and floating along with the strong current. The only way to stop was to grab one of the ropes tied to the pier and then shinny up the poles back onto the dock. The East River had been very polluted, but we hadn't minded—just as long as we got cooled off.

By the beginning of grade nine, I had had no time for school at all anymore. The gang had become my whole way of life.

At Elmira, I attended a grade eight class taught by a civilian from the town. He was a white man, tall and skinny and plain looking. He lectured the class and if nobody was paying attention, he didn't care—he just went on talking. I listened off and on, but I found most of the subjects difficult and boring. They seemed unnecessary; they didn't relate to my own experience at all. My mind drifted. I found it hard to concentrate on geography and history and the other subjects. My attitude was generally poor and unreceptive; I was there just to "do" my time and wasn't interested in learning.

The one good thing about school was that I met Sanchez there. He sat at the desk across the aisle from me, a quiet eighteen-year-old Puerto Rican about the same medium height and weight as myself.

One day he was having trouble with some math problems that the teacher had given us to solve.

"Hey, you know how to do this stuff, man?" he asked me, frustrated.

"Yeah," I answered. "It's easy. There's nothin' to it." When it came to fraction problems, I was able to solve most of them. Math was one of my better subjects.

"Can you help me, man?" Sanchez asked. "I'm stuck."

"Sure, why not?" I responded, taking an immediate liking to the youth. After that we became friends.

Sanchez and I had a lot in common. He had been involved in a gang and had been arrested for robbery. He was a loner like me. In our free time, we just naturally chummed around together. We often talked about the "streets" and rock 'n roll music, discovering that we both enjoyed the same groups. When we had our hour of exercise in the yard in the late afternoon, Sanchez and I would often sit in the baseball bleachers and fool around with "do-wah-booms" and "la-la-las." Before long, we had a good harmony going between us. Usually a few other inmates would be spread out across the stands in small groups, singing, playing guitars, or just listening.

After lunch I went to the carpentry workshop. Every day I sat down on a bench at the large table with the other men, who were all involved in making chairs. The civilian carpenter, a man in his late fifties, patiently trained me in the skill of chair-making. First I had to select four suitable maplewood boards and glue the sides together to serve as a seat. After the glue dried, the next step was to draw the shape of a seat, from a cardboard pattern onto the wood's surface, and saw around it. Then, using various chisels, I carved out the contour of the seat to make it comfortable to sit on. This procedure took me many months to complete. If I had wanted to, I could have had the entire chair finished in two months, but I wasn't very enthusiastic about the project. I was going as slowly as possible, just trying to kill time. Sometimes I interrupted the work on my chair to fix broken stools—just for a diversion; and at other times, I hung around the shop, watching the other men's progress. Every now and then, the carpenter came around to check our work and offer helpful suggestions.

"How's it coming, Narvaez?" he would ask me cheerfully.

"OK, I guess," I would always shrug. He would examine my chair and correct me if necessary.

He didn't mind that it was taking me so long to complete the seat—after all, what was the hurry?

After I finally finished carving out the seat, I sanded it down—which took up a few more months. The next stage, the most difficult, was the carving of the leg spindles. This was done by holding a chisel against the leg which was attached to a spinning lathe wheel. At this point, I made many mistakes. Sometimes I found that I had carved the leg out of proportion, with one area too thin and another too thick. Or else the chisel would slip in my hands and cut right across the leg, breaking it in half.

I had to throw many legs away before I made four half-decent ones. These I glued into the holes I had whittled on the bottom of the seat. That's as far as I ever got. I never reached the stage of attaching the back of the chair. In the entire year and a half that I spent at Elmira, I succeeded in completing the bottom portion of exactly one chair. I wasn't the fastest worker!

TWELVE
Disappointment

When the parole board hearings were due at Elmira, there was a general excitement among the prison population. A little hope stirred within the heart of even the most cynical and hardened of the criminals. Afterward, however, it was a different story. . . .

When I had been at Elmira for a year and a half, after serving two and a half years of my sentence altogether, a guard delivered an envelope to my cell. The letter inside stated that I was to appear—finally—before the parole review committee.

"Don't set your expectations too high," Sanchez warned me one afternoon as we walked over to our usual place in the bleachers. "You've got a mean crime hanging over your head—and they're not gonna turn you loose—yet."

"Yeah, man, you're right," I sighed in resignation. Realistically, my chances of being released on parole were very slim—about one in a thousand. Sanchez's friendly warning had deflated me—but try as I might, I couldn't relinquish my hope altogether. There was always that chance. . . .

"Good luck, man," I called to Sanchez on the day of the scheduled hearings. He was also up for parole review and I knew that his chances were much better than mine.

I entered the room reserved for the parole board hearings, braced for disappointment. The three members of the committee, two men and one woman, were sitting around a table, deeply engrossed in examining my records. They didn't look up as I sat down on the only available chair, placed directly in front of them. I cracked my knuckles nervously.

At last one of the men looked up.

"What have you been doing since you've been here, Mr. Narvaez?" He was gazing at a spot on the wall somewhere over my head.

"Going to school," I shrugged. "And to the carpentry shop."

"What have you made in that time at the shop?" the other man inquired.

"A chair," I said.

There was an awkward pause. No one smiled.

"One chair?" he raised his eyebrows quizzically.

"Yes, sir."

"In over a year and a half, you've made one chair?" he peered at me harshly.

"Yes, sir," I mumbled. I could tell from their expressions that I was in trouble.

"Well, it doesn't appear that you've accomplished much in the past year, Mr. Narvaez," the woman said coldly, eyeing me sternly from behind her glasses. She seemed to be even more unsympathetic than the men.

After that the interview went from bad to worse. The committee members remained solemn and aloof. They shot questions at me, and then without paying attention to what I was saying or sometimes not even waiting for me to finish, they asked more. It didn't take me long to figure out that they were going through the whole procedure strictly as a matter of routine. They had already made their decision—and I doubted if it was in my favor.

"Mr. Narvaez," the woman asked me as the session was drawing to a close, "what do you plan to do after you are released?"

"I dunno," I shrugged, my arms crossed defensively over my chest. The question had caught me off guard.

"Don't you think you had better start giving your future some serious thought?" she said crisply, an air of finality in her voice.

"Yes, ma'am," I muttered, but I was thinking bitterly, "I've got plenty of time to think about that—that's all I've got—time. . . ."

"You may go now, Mr. Narvaez," the man informed me, not bothering to rise.

I stood up, confused. I was still in the dark about their decision. "Well, do I get parole?" I asked bluntly, wanting to get the bad news over with.

"We're sorry, Mr. Narvaez. We're not at liberty to tell you at this time. We've got forty more men to interview before the day is over and then we'll make our final decision. . . ."

"When do I find out, then?" I inquired impatiently.

"Tonight," he informed me curtly. "You'll receive an envelope containing everything you want to know."

"Yeah, I bet," I thought to myself cynically, closing the door behind me. "Tonight, after you're safely off the grounds and miles away from here, then I'll find out—then, when there's no chance of "thanking" you for your decision. . . ."

Around midnight a guard brought me the long-awaited envelope. I ripped it open, then stared blankly at the words,

PAROLE HAS BEEN DENIED TO MR. ISRAEL NARVAEZ.

I read no further. Instead, I crumpled the paper up in my hand and threw it out between the bars as far as I could. I lay awake on my mattress far into the night, cursing that parole board committee with every curse word I knew.

The next day Sanchez was jubilant.

"Guess what, man?" he cried. I knew what he was going to say. "I'm getting turned loose!"

"That's cool, man," I was genuinely happy for him.

"Baby, I've been waiting a long long time for this day—" he slapped his fist into his palm.

"I know . . . " I scuffed my toe against the ground.

"Hey listen, man, it's too bad—" Sanchez suddenly became conscious of me.

"Aw, forget it," I shrugged. "I knew I didn't stand a chance."

"Well, maybe next time." He tried to cheer me.

"Yeah, maybe," I answered pessimistically, then quickly changed the subject, "Hey, when are you cuttin' loose from this joint?"

"Man, as soon as I can! But I have to get a job first. It's one of the conditions of my parole. But, baby—that's no problem," he said confidently. Nothing could crush his enthusiasm today.

A few weeks later, I sat with Sanchez in the baseball bleachers for the last time. We talked about his plans. His parents, who lived in Manhattan, had found him a job as a delivery boy. He was excited about his departure early the next morning, about walking through those high gates and never looking back.

"Maybe we'll see each other on the outside," Sanchez was saying. "Then we could get hunched up together and sing. We'll call ourselves 'Sanchez and Narvaez'—or maybe, 'Narvaez and Sanchez'? Sounds good, huh?"

"Yeah," I answered slowly, "maybe we'll do that. . . ."

There wasn't time for a long farewell. We crossed the exercise yard to return to our cells.

"Well, catch you later, man," Sanchez said as we parted.

I slapped his palm. "Yeah. Good luck, man." I watched him disappear among a throng of inmates.

Shortly after Sanchez's departure, I was informed that I was being transferred to another prison—one for hardened criminals. The parole board committee must have decided that I was not showing any signs of rehabilitation or progress or improvement.

In the morning, a guard escorted me to a cell in solitary confinement. The solitary confinement cells were a few levels underground, at the very bottom of the prison complex: they were dark, cold, and damp. I was locked in there overnight. The following morning a group of us were loaded onto a bus. I had no idea where I was going, but if I had, I wouldn't have been so anxious for a change of scenery.

THIRTEEN
Reunion

I had just settled down for the evening in my new cell at the Great Meadows Correctional Institute, more commonly known as the Comstock State Penitentiary, when a shadowed visitor came and stood in front of my cell.

"*Pssssttt. . . .*"

"What now?" I muttered to myself, keeping my eyes closed and lying very still. I pretended to be asleep, hoping he would go away and leave me alone. But it was no use.

"Hey, you, number twelve!" he rattled the bars impatiently.

I slid my feet over the side of the mattress, shading my eyes against the light to see who my unwelcome visitor was. I recognized the pencil-slim silhouette as that of the young Negro water boy, who had made his rounds earlier in the evening, carrying hot water from cell to cell. Tonight I had only taken enough water to make a cup of coffee, but other nights I had my bucket filled so I could wash my underwear—which, due to the grave shortage of such garments in prison, would quickly disappear if I sent them to the laundry.

"Whadya want?" I asked the boy irritably.

"I've got a lil' present for you. . . ."

"Yeah?" I said suspiciously. Nobody gives you anything in prison without expecting something in return. This news could mean only one thing. Trouble. "What is it?"

"Come on over and see for yourself, man."

With all my senses alert, I approached the bars. The boy grinned, his white teeth gleaming in his shadowed face. In one hand, he held an empty aluminum five-gallon water can, and in the other, a plain brown paper bag.

"Here," he thrust the paper bag at me.

"What's in it?" I asked cautiously, refusing to take it.

"Take a look." He held the bag up to my face so that I could examine its contents.

The bag contained a couple of oranges and an apple.

"Hey, who gave these to you?" I snapped.

The water boy shrugged. "Some dude."

"Man, I don't know any dudes here," I barked at him, trying to outshout the cold fear that gripped my insides. Somebody somewhere in this prison was challenging my manhood. This gift of fruit was nothing less than a sexual offering. "You made a mistake, jack. Take that back where it came from. I don't want it."

"I can't do that, man," he almost whined.

"You better," I growled fiercely. "If you know what's good for you!"

"C'mon, man," he pleaded. "Give me a break, huh? Take it. It's yours. Your buddy sent it."

"I told you, I ain't got no buddies in this joint. You tell this jerk just where he can go!" I was more angry than frightened by now.

"Well, he says he's your pal," the boy persisted. "And I ain't gonna walk all around to the other side of the tier again and hand these fruits back to him. No way! I ain't that crazy!"

I swore. "What's this son of a — look like?" I decided to pump this kid for as much information as I could—it paid to know who your enemies were. Inside, I was feeling sick. From now on, I would have to be doubly on the alert. I would never know just when my admirer would choose to attack: in the exercise yard . . . a dark hall . . . the workshop . . . the showers. I would be in constant danger.

The boy thought for a moment. "Oh, he's a tall dude. And sorta Chinese-lookin', you know?"

That had me puzzled. I couldn't recall any man of that description eyeing me in the mess hall when I'd gone for supper. But of course, in a crowd of that size he could have easily watched me without me noticing him.

"Listen, what's this dude's name? What do they call him?"

"Lemme think now," the boy scratched his head. "I've heard it somewhere. Cato? . . . Cade? No . . . Carl? Carl! That's it," he grinned happily. "Carl."

"Carl!" I shouted with relief, my fear evaporating instantly. "Carl! Man, why didn't you say so in the first place?"

Carl was Chino's proper name. Good old Chino. Would I be glad to see him again!

"Everything's cool," I told the water boy. "I'll take the fruit." He handed the bag of fruit over to me and vanished.

I sank down on my mattress and stared at the fruit, shaking my head in amazement. My mind was still on my recent fright. I sighed heavily and wiped my sweaty palms on my trousers. After awhile, I picked out a fat orange and peeled it carefully, enjoying every moment. With exquisite delight, I popped the juicy sections into my mouth. They tasted slightly sour, but boy were they good! It had been ages since I had been treated to fresh fruit. The commissary didn't sell it and visitors weren't allowed to bring any into the compound—the authorities were afraid that drugs would be injected into the soft pulp.

"Trust Chino to smuggle these in." I smiled to myself, sucking on a particularly juicy section. "He's up to his old tricks . . . Man, it's gonna be good to see him again!"

It had been over a year and a half since we had parted.

"Maybe Comstock's not gonna be so bad, after all," I grinned. "Not with Chino here to show me the ropes. . . ."

I saw Chino the next morning. At breakfast, I was seated at a table with the other men from reception, when I spotted him coming through the doors at the far end of the mess hall with his tier group. As he shuffled along in the food line, I waved to him and he waved back.

"Hey, what's happening, man?" I mouthed the words silently to him, across the rows of inmates between us.

Chino smiled and shrugged.

That moment was like a miracle to me. It gave me a warm, wonderful feeling to see somebody I knew—a friend—among all those scowling strangers. When a convict first arrives at a new prison—I don't care how many prisons he's been through—he is raked with fear of the unknown. After being lulled by a familiar routine, it is unnerving, even terrifying, for him to suddenly face change. That's how I had felt, but now, seeing Chino eased my fears.

Unfortunately, we were not allowed to talk to each other. I was in "reception" and Chino was in "general population." From a distance, I watched him. He sat with his tier group at their regular table and wolfed down his food, joking between mouthfuls with the men on either side of him.

"Same old Chino," I thought to myself fondly, loyalty surging up within me. "He hasn't changed one bit." It appeared that he had faced up to his twenty-year sentence bravely, taking it in his stride. He had molded himself into the routine, adapting to the prison system as well as anyone could. Prison life almost agreed with him.

"Well, there ain't no sense in him crying over spilt milk," I concluded philosophically. "We all just gotta do our time. . . . me, Chino, every-body."

On the first day when I was transferred to "general population," a Puerto Rican, whom I recognized as one of Chino's friends, was sitting at the next table over from mine at lunch.

Near the end of the meal, he swung around on his bench and called over to me: "Hey, man, Chino wants to see you. When it's time to go to the Big Yard, go to court number sixteen. OK?"

"Cool," I responded, giving him the thumbs up sign. I had no idea what court number sixteen was, but I would soon find out.

When I went to the Big Yard for exercise, I kept my eyes peeled for Chino. This was the free time period for all the inmates at Comstock; everyone could do what he wanted. A lot of the men stood around in small groups, smoking and shooting the breeze or just staring absently into space. Others played baseball while the less energetic ones watched from the bleachers.

The Big Yard, as all the cons referred to it, really was large—the size of a couple of football fields, at least. I asked around in order to locate court sixteen, which turned out to be a handball court. There were thirty or forty of these handball courts located against one of the walls surrounding the exercise yard. Chino and his gang spent all of their free time hanging around the courts, waiting for a turn to play.

Chino was easy to spot; he was head and shoulders above the other Puerto Ricans with him. I made my way eagerly over to him.

"Hey, man, how are you?" he greeted me with equal enthusiasm. "Give me five."

"OK. What's happening?" We slapped each other's palms.

"Nothing much," Chino grinned, revealing even, white teeth. "I've been rotting away in this stinkhole forever. Hey, guys," he waved over a few of the other Puerto Ricans who were standing around. "I want you to meet my crime partner, Israel."

"Cool," they said, slapping my palms. Then they went back to watching the handball games.

"What's this joint like, man?" I asked Chino seriously.

"Aw—all right," he shrugged. "If you stick with us you won't have any problems. . . ."

"Right," I said soberly, having a good idea of the problems he was referring to. "Hey, thanks for the fruit. They were good—but wow, man, did they give me a scare!"

"Yeah?" his handsome face creased with amusement. "How come?"

"I thought some dude had taken a liking to me, you know what I mean? Wanted to turn me into a trick and all that junk," I answered, kicking the pavement. "And I ain't ever gonna be nobody's trick!"

"Yeah, you always gotta keep a lookout for perverts around here," Chino warned me. "Things happen all the time. . . ." He was lost in his own thoughts for a few moments, but suddenly he turned his attention back to the handball courts. One game was just finishing.

"Hey, Chino. You're up," a Puerto Rican called from the sidelines.

"You wanna game?" Chino asked me, anxious to play.

"With you? You kiddin'?" I laughed. I had never played handball before in my life. "No way! You're too good for me. You go ahead and I'll watch. Maybe I'll pick up some tips."

"OK, man. Catch you later."

To my surprise, as I wandered around the Big Yard, I actually bumped into three or four guys I had known back in Brooklyn. Two of them were from the Hellburners, a brother gang, and another was Johnny, a tall, light-skinned Puerto Rican and a fellow MauMau. We had hung around together a lot in the old days. We had eaten at each other's homes and I knew his sister and he knew my brothers. I spent most of my free time with Chino, Alfredo, Johnny, and the two Hellburners. Because of our common background and mutual interests, we naturally formed a close allegiance with one another. It felt good to have a few friends in the prison, people I could trust.

With the other prisoners, I was always cautious. I never relaxed my defenses. I trusted no one. When I walked down the corridors, I walked in fear, my hands ready at my sides, my fists tightly clenched, always aware that at any moment a con could spring on me. Week after week, there were fresh rumors about the latest victim of attack. Sometimes the victims had been grabbed from behind and their throats slit from ear to ear with a rusty razor blade or a jagged piece of piping. Sometimes their faces had been slashed or they had been stuck in the back with a knife. The "knives" in Comstock were actually long nails that had been flattened out and crudely sharpened to a deadly point.

And then there were those who had been raped. These unfortunate men were easy to pick out. They walked around in a self-induced trance, heads hanging, spirits broken. Overnight, their personalities changed. They couldn't accept what had happened to them; they were ashamed of themselves. They were like the walking dead. In the eyes of the other cons, they were outcasts. They were now branded "tricks."

One evening I got to talking with my neighbor in the next cell.

"What you doin' here, man? What you get busted for?" I asked him more out of boredom than curiosity.

"I killed my girl friend."

"Yeah? How come?"

"Found her with another guy," he answered glumly. "So I killed her. Stabbed her with a kitchen knife. Twenty times."

A lot of the inmates at Comstock were like my neighbor. They were tough, silent, morose, locked within themselves. It was the only way you could be. Prison is a struggle for survival, and only the toughest survive.

Some of the inmates didn't care whether they survived or not. They were apathetic, not caring what happened to them anymore. Fat and sluggish, they walked around aimlessly like sagging hunks of flesh. An interminable sentence stretched before them; they resigned themselves to prison life, losing all desire, all hope. They weren't living anymore—they were merely existing.

As time passed, I grew more and more like the men around me. I became withdrawn, sullen, bitter. You can't live with animals, eat with them, sleep with them, without becoming one yourself. Evil breeds rapidly. As we were so fond of quoting to one another: "Behind these prison walls goes a certain verse: The good man grows evil and the evil grows worse."

FOURTEEN
The Hole

As the months passed in Comstock, I found that I was getting involved in more fights. This was partly because I wanted to gain a solid reputation as a tough guy and partly because I was bored and frustrated. Fighting was a good way of letting off steam.

Most of my fights began over silly things. They broke out easily and quickly and on the slightest provocation. Afterward, half of the time, I couldn't even remember what had caused them. A good case in point is one of the fights I had with my friend Johnny. . . .

During our free time period, Johnny and I chummed around together a lot. One afternoon when we were joking around in the Big Yard, we got a little loose with our hands. At first we were just playfully punching each other, but then the punches became harder, and before we knew it, we were fighting in earnest.

Immediately, two of the guards on duty rushed over to pull us apart.

"All right, guys. Break it up."

"Cool it."

As the guards marched us off to our cells, I rubbed my bruised cheek and dabbed at my cut, swollen lip. We had both managed to get a few good swings in before the guards separated us, but fortunately, neither of us was seriously injured.

Johnny and I were locked in our cells until the following afternoon when an appointment was made for us to meet with the lieutenant. In the meantime, the guards filed a report on the fight and attached "keep locked" notices beside our cell numbers on the master switch control. We were not allowed to leave our cells for supper that night nor for breakfast in the morning. Instead an inmate brought a meal tray to our cells.

The next day, the lieutenant questioned us one at a time so that we each had the chance to tell our own version of the fight. He was a huge man, 6'6" and 300 pounds, and he used his enormous size to intimidate the inmates.

"OK, Narvaez. Tell me what happened," the lieutenant ordered as he leaned back in his swivel chair, his flabby bulk spread out before him.

One of the unwritten prisoners' codes is that you don't rat on a fellow con. In this case there was no question of ratting.

"Ain't much to tell, sir," I told him honestly. "One minute we were just fooling around and the next minute we were fighting."

The lieutenant looked at me, his face an expressionless mask. I couldn't tell what was going on in his mind. He tapped his pen on his knee and waited. He had me where he wanted me—right under his thumb.

"C'mon, Narvaez," he mocked me. "you can do better than that."

"No, sir," I said, poker-faced. "That's the truth."

The lieutenant clicked his ball point pen. "How did the fighting start?"

"I dunno," I replied blandly. "It just started."

Now he didn't play any tricks with me; he came straight to the point.

"Fighting is against the regulations," he informed me, needlessly. "You'll have to pay the penalty."

"Yes, sir."

"You'll be locked in solitary confinement for a few days—to cool off."

"Yes, sir."

I was hustled out of the lieutenant's office and taken to a special wing of the prison complex—all the cons referred to it as the "Hole." A guard ordered me to strip, and took away my denim jeans and workshirt, leaving me in nothing but my shorts.

It was cold in the cell—part of the punishing process. Shivering, I paced back and forth, rubbing my arms for warmth. When I got tired of pacing, I did a few pushups and then ran up and down on the spot, trying to work up a sweat. Afterward, however, I only felt colder.

The cell contained only a sink and crude toilet in one corner. There was no bed to lie down on.

At night, a guard would throw a smelly mattress onto the floor, a mattress reeking of urine. But in the daytime, I did not have even that debatable comfort. Instead, I had to sit down on the cold cement floor, leaning my back against the steel wall. After a few hours of sitting like that in silence, cracking my knuckles, I called out miserably:

"Hey, Johnny, you there?"

There was a long pause, and then, from somewhere down the hall, came the dry, muffled reply, "Yeah, I'm here." After the unbearable silence, I had never heard anything so wonderful as that human voice.

"Hey, man, what you hit me for?" I feigned anger.

"I dunno. What you hit me for?"

We both laughed.

"Beats me," I shrugged. "What are we doin' here, anyway?" At this stage, the fight seemed ridiculous.

"Man, what a bunch of chumps we are. . . ."

Finally, a few days later, we were returned to our own cells. The first thing I did was to stretch out on my mattress—such luxury. I never thought I would see the day when I would be happy to be locked up in this cell, but it sure beat the Hole. Here, at least, I had food in my locker, fresh clothes to change into, and hot water at night.

And in a way, this cell of mine had become "home" to me. I had fixed it up and it now bore my personal touch. By ripping up some sheets my mother had sent me, I had created a fancy covering to go around the rim of my lidless toilet, making it nicer to look at. I also had a pair of braided scatter-rugs spread across the floor, which I had bought from a departing inmate; and a stool in one corner, which I often moved around for variety's sake.

In the Big Yard the following day, Johnny and I just naturally drifted together, and soon we were laughing and joking as if the fight between us had never occurred. We were still good buddies.

For days after, however, other inmates would not let me forget the incident. "Hey, man," they would rib me, "I heard you fought your best friend." Everybody knew everything that was going on. Living in that prison was like living in a small town; gossip spread fast.

That fight with Johnny had not been my first one and neither would it be my last. Generally I tried to keep the delicate balance between fighting too much and not fighting enough. If an inmate went looking for trouble, he would find it, all right; everyone and his brother would want to take him on. I had to be willing to fight if the need arose, but try not to provoke the fights. I kept a low profile.

The inmates at Comstock were roughly divided into social groups—prison had its own society. Besides the distinct ethnic groups, there were groups within groups: big city boys and country hicks, fighters and "flunkies," "straights" and "tricks." Like naturally attracted like. It was hard to say how each prisoner knew the group to which he belonged; he depended on a silent signal, a mutual understanding, or a certain look in the eye.

Most of the guys I hung around with were very much like me, of similar background and outlook. We were known as fighters and were respected by the other inmates; nobody messed around with us. During our time in the yard, we would often sit in the bleachers and watch Chino and the others playing handball.

Another group of inmates—very different from us—would also be sharing the bleachers, clustered together in little groups, reading or discussing books. These men were the prison intellectuals, the philosophers, the political radicals. I had often been curious about these men and one afternoon when I was alone, I approached a Puerto Rican, who was intently poring over a book.

"Hey, man, whatcha reading?" I asked him.

He appraised me. "Plato. Plato and Marx."

I shrugged. I had heard the names before but they meant nothing to me. "They any good?"

"Yeah," the Puerto Rican said drily. "They're good, all right. They've got some pretty interesting things to say. . . ."

"Yeah," I said. "Like what?"

"Like about the system."

"System?" I repeated dumbly. "What system?" I was confused.

"Our system. The American system. The capitalist system," he almost shouted. "Man, get with it!"

"What's wrong with our system?" I inquired innocently.

"Man, everything!" he exclaimed angrily. "The

rich people get richer and the poor people get poorer. Our whole society's stacked in favor of the rich man. How many rich dudes have you met in here? Hardly any, right? If a rich dude commits a crime, he gets himself the best lawyer money can buy and he gets off scott free, right?"

I nodded. What he was saying made sense.

"But," he spit the words out like watermelon seeds, "if a poor Negro or Latin, like me or you, commits the same crime, what do we get?"

I shrugged.

"Five. Ten. Twenty years. See what I mean? The rich dudes get all the breaks. Take yourself, for instance," he said, calming down. "Where you from?"

"Brooklyn."

"The ghetto, right?"

I shrugged. I had never heard that word before. The world I had grown up in was the only world I knew. . . .

"And what you get busted for?"

"A gang murder. . . ."

"How many years you get?"

"Five."

"Five, huh? How many years you think you would have got if you had the best criminal lawyer in New York City working on your case?"

"I dunno," I shrugged. I had never given the matter much thought.

"Well, I'll tell you," he said fervently. "None! That's right. Zippo. The more you pay for a lawyer, the better deal you're gonna get. It's a fact of life. Ask anybody here. He'll tell you the same thing!"

The more I listened to this man, known as one of the "jailhouse lawyers," the angrier I became. What he said burned me up. My frustration and wrath were becoming directed against the society that had put me behind bars:

"Man, if I had had money," I thought to myself bitterly, "I wouldn't be in this joint. . . ."

I began to spend more and more of my free time with these intellectuals. Most of them were Negroes and Puerto Ricans, and most were dope addicts, arrested on robbery charges while trying to support their habit. The other inmates tended to think of these men as weirdos who spent their yard time discussing crazy ideas when they could be exercising. But to me, they seemed to know what they were talking about, and I listened, fascinated. They made me think about things I had never thought about before; challenged me to question things that I had never questioned. They talked about Communism a great deal. In communist countries, they said, everybody was equal, nobody was better than anybody else, nobody went to bed hungry, and nobody was on welfare.

Sensing my growing interest, these men loaned me some of their books written by Marx. Dutifully, I tried to read them, but I had difficulty understanding them so I had to ask them to explain the books to me, and they did. And what they said sounded good to me. Slowly, they were convincing me that Communism promised a better way of life than the one I had known. I wavered in that direction. . . .

FIFTEEN
Marking Time

Several months later, around midnight, I was lying wide awake on my mattress; for some reason I was having trouble falling asleep. I tossed and turned restlessly.

"*Aaaaiiiieeeeeeee . . .*" an ear-piercing shriek echoed through the cell block.

I sat bolt upright. What on earth was going on? It sounded like some poor inmate was being tortured.

"*Aaaaiiieeeeee . . .*" the screaming continued, now more of a long drawn-out wail, rising and falling in volume.

There was something eerie about that scream. Something violent and primitive. It gave me the shivers. I listened for sounds of a scuffle that would accompany a beating, but could hear none. All at once I knew that the scream was not a protest against physical pain, but of some private inner torment. The poor jerk was "cracking up."

From somewhere in the cell block, I heard the clank of a cell door opening. The screaming suddenly died. A muffled moaning sound, retreating footsteps, and then all was quiet. The silence was even more terrifying. . . .

I lay quite still on my bed. I could not forget that cry of anguish. It haunted me. In my mind, I could hear the inmate's crazed screams again, could almost hear his very senses escaping out of his mouth—reality, like a spirit, departing from him forever. It frightened me. I knew that tomorrow, or the next day, or the day after that, the same thing could happen to me. My mind might just snap. It took me a long time to fall asleep after that. . . .

Sometimes I was sure that I was going insane myself. It wasn't so bad out in the Big Yard or in the mess hall, but when I was locked up in my cell for the evening, all alone with my own thoughts, that's when it was the worst. That's when I wondered what my life would have been like if I hadn't been mixed up in a murder.

"Would I be a drug addict by now?" I mused.

"Or a successful businessman?"

"Maybe a rock 'n roll singer?"

"Would I be married?"

"Would I be in college?"

"Or maybe dead, stabbed in some dark alley?"

Sometimes I would wake up in a cold sweat, shaking. I would have nightmares about the night of the killing. Vividly, I would see Chino raise the gun . . . see the Angel falling . . . his eyes popping . . . blood spattering. . . .

And then I would think of hell. I hadn't

thought of hell in a long time, but I thought about it now. . . .

"Aw, hell can't be much worse than this joint." I would try to shrug off my fears. "Prison's a hell. Same thing day in, day out, year in, year out. Like Chinese torture. No wonder guys crack up!" Nobody ever gets used to doing time. Nobody.

At nights, lying on my bed in the darkness, I would stare, as if hypnotized, at the bars in front of me. Sometimes it felt as though those bars were closing in on me, choking me . . . burning right through me, searing my flesh. Even when I closed my eyes, I could feel their presence, their shadows upon my body. Would I ever be out of their reach?

I went through various periods of mental instability. Sometimes these periods would be triggered when I received news from home—especially bad news. Once, my older brother Manny was stabbed by a jealous man in a fight over a girl, the girl Manny was engaged to marry. That set me on edge for a week. Another time, my mother was hit by a car and taken to the hospital. Fortunately, she suffered only a broken leg, but the accident shook me up. If anything had happened to my mother . . . !

I tried not to think too much or to let my thoughts stray very far from prison. To think of my mother, my family, my home became unbearable.

Instead I tried to keep myself busy with meaningless tasks. I marked the passing days off in my calendar. I counted the days I had left to serve.

The hours. The minutes. Sometimes I just stared blankly at the bars and counted them too. My mental ability with arithmetic improved considerably.

Each evening before I went to bed, I performed a series of pushups and other exercises on the floor of my cell. With so much time on my hands to devote to physical fitness, I kept my body firm and in good shape. The workouts had an extra benefit too. Self-defense. If you looked muscular, the other inmates would think twice about tackling you. Strength meant something in prison.

The worst time of the year for any prisoner is Christmas. As the Christmas season approached, in contrast to the merry hustle and bustle of excitement that usually characterizes this time of year, the atmosphere at Comstock grew increasingly heavy and depressed, anything but joyful. Tempers flared. Fights broke out. Everyone became emotionally unstable: moody, touchy, easily upset.

Two weeks before Christmas, my parents paid me an unexpected visit. My mother hadn't been able to make it up for the last few months—it seemed more like years. But it was seeing my father that surprised me the most. This was one of his rare visits.

"How you doing?" he greeted me stiffly, allowing no trace of emotion to show in his voice. Men must behave like men. . . .

"OK," I replied in the same even tone.

"How are they treating you?" he asked gruffly

and coughed. It was an attempt at conversation, anyway.

"OK," I shrugged. What could I say?

"Been doing anything new?" he inquired, at a loss for anything better to say.

"Nah. Same old routine. Nothing changes around here. How about you? Are you off on another trip?"

He nodded. "The day after Christmas. Africa this time."

"Oh."

My father had traveled all over the world as a seaman for the Merchant Marines. As a kid, I had rarely seen him. He was always coming and going. When his ship sailed into New York, he would slip into the house late at night when we were all asleep. A few days later he would slip off again in the early hours of the morning before anyone was up. His destination—unknown. I had never understood my father, nor he me. We had nothing in common. His world was a strange, exotic one to me—all those foreign places. The streets of the ghetto were the only world I knew. We had never gotten to know each other.

My mother, putting up a brave front, chatted away nervously (she was always nervous at first) about all the news from home. Most of it didn't mean anything to me. I had been out of that world for so long that its petty carryings-on held no interest for me. Not that they ever really had . . . my brothers' and sisters' faces were only hazy blurs in my mind. Even when we had been under the same roof, we had never had much to do with each other. We had all been caught up in our own private affairs, wrapped up in our own isolated little worlds. Not much love had been lost among us.

Before they left, my parents gave me a package.

"Your Christmas present," my mother said, about to burst into tears. She hugged me, my father shook my hand, and then they were gone.

Back in my cell, I slowly untied the package. Inside I found all sorts of tins of food, mostly canned fruit and candies. The authorities had given my mother a list of all the items she was allowed to bring to me and she had picked out everything she knew I would enjoy. Looking at the cans of food, chosen with love, I felt a lump in my throat.

On the morning before Christmas, I was lying on my cot feeling particularly blue. I had never been one to make a fuss over Christmas, but now I grew quite sentimental about it. Knowing that everyone else in the outside world would be celebrating and partying made being locked up behind bars a thousand times worse than usual.

"Man, bet you everybody is having a good time, drinking and eating," I muttered in misery and envy, feeling quite sorry for myself.

Everyone would be spending Christmas with loved ones. Suddenly I wanted nothing more than to be with mine. I missed all my brothers and sisters, my mother and my father, as I had never missed them before. A great wave of loneliness engulfed me. I pictured my mother sitting by the tree, crying because I wasn't there to open my presents. I imagined the pain she would be going through at this time tomorrow.

I had only snatched a few winks of sleep all night, so troubling were my thoughts. Now as dawn approached, I was just drifting off into a light sleep when I got the surprise of my life!

All the cell doors suddenly grated open. Guards paraded up and down the catwalk below, shouting:

"All prisoners, remove your clothes at once and step outside your cells!"

What on earth was going on? What could this mean?

I obeyed the order and stood shivering on the catwalk outside my cell. The guards had often conducted surprise raids, searching the cells for dangerous weapons. (They were usually not too successful in catching anybody because as soon as the inmates heard the guards coming, they hastily threw their weapons on the cell roof. Of course, the guards cleared the roof afterward, but they couldn't pin the rap on anybody.) But this morning, this was no routine raid. The guards thoroughly searched each cell, confiscating all sorts of things, such as bottles and jars, which they normally allowed us to keep in our cupboards.

"Man, what are they up to?" I grumbled, perplexed. "Why are they taking my jar of mayonnaise?" I soon found out why. . . .

On Christmas morning, in what seemed to be a custom, all of the convicts leaped from their beds, grabbed hold of the movable portion of their cell doors, and shook the bars violently.

Anything that made noise, they shook and banged. The deafening noise echoed and reechoed in the vast cavernous space surrounding the tier blocks.

"Man, what a racket!" I cried, caught up in the emotional excitement. To me it sounded like the rattling of a thousand bones. It set my teeth on edge and gave me the shivers, but I joined in with the rest of them.

Bottles and jars and other breakable objects (which some cons had managed to hide) were hurled from cells on the various tier levels and they crashed on the cement floor far below. The floor was literally covered in shattered fragments of glass.

On New Year's Eve, the whole commotion was repeated again. I grabbed those bars and shook them as if I thought I could break them apart. Everyone screamed:

"Happy New Year! Happy New Year!"

I shouted those words as if I thought I could be heard above all the din. I harbored no illusions that the coming year—my final year—would bring me any happiness. If it was going to be anything like the last four I had endured, I had nothing but more suffering ahead. But still I shouted those magic three words until I thought my lungs would burst:

"Happy New Year!"

SIXTEEN
Parole

During the day, for eight long hours, I worked in the carpentry shop. (Actually, I wouldn't really call it "working"—it was more like sitting.) At the shop in Elmira we had made chairs, but here at Comstock, all we did was repair broken stools. When there weren't any stools to fix—which was usually the case—everybody would just sit around and talk. It was a soft job.

Chino had a soft job, too. He worked in the barber shop. In the three years that he had been at Comstock, he had developed into a very capable barber—and he enjoyed cutting hair. Whenever a guard ordered me to get my hair trimmed (we could never wear it below our ears) I usually asked for Chino. As always, he was very fast with his hands:

Snip. Snip. Snip. The scissors flashed silver.

"Hey, man. Watch it!" I would joke around with him. "Don't cut my ears off!"

"Aw, don't worry about it," Chino would scoff. "Or I might cut your throat while I'm at it."

"Yeah, baby, you just try!"

Some of the inmates, however, didn't want the soft jobs. They preferred the jobs that required muscle. The men who were responsible for washing the floors, for instance, liked to build up their bodies as they worked. Grunting, they would swing the heavy dripping mops from one hand to the other across the floor in steady rhythm, like a horse's tail swishing flies. As a result of their effort, these men proudly displayed broad shoulders and chest.

On slow afternoons in the carpentry shop, we would-be carpenters sat around the tables and talked. One of the men I most often talked with was a tall good-looking Puerto Rican from the Bronx named David. David was a dope addict who had gone cold turkey a long time ago, but he was still very nervous and fidgety. Whenever he rolled up his sleeves on hot days, his badly blotched veins gave his past away. His skin was a sickly yellow color too—as if he was suffering from a bout of jaundice or meningitis.

David and I gradually became good friends—something which doesn't happen very often between inmates who didn't know each other on the outside. (I, for example had many "acquaintances" but few "friends.") We talked about our past experiences, our crimes, the streets, and our families. He told me that he had a wife and kid, and although he didn't tell me directly—a subject like this was too personal for him to discuss with me—I soon discovered that he was separated. A lot of the men at Comstock were bitter because their wives had divorced them while they were serving time. Usually they received a "Dear John" letter and word soon circulated that so-and-so's "old lady" had cut him loose.

Another inmate I frequently talked with in the carpentry shop was Pete. Pete had belonged to a Manhattan gang and was also doing time for shooting a rival gang member. I had first seen him at the Atlantic Detention Home and later at Elmira, but it was only since he had been transferred to Comstock that we had really talked. It was good to see an old face. (Pete had a chubby round face and black "porcupine" hair that stuck straight up.) We felt an immediate affinity for one another.

One day when we were sitting idly around the tables, I casually asked him:

"Hey, man, where do you live?"

"Prospect Avenue," he answered, giving me his exact address.

"Yeah? That's cool. My parents don't live too far from there. Only three or four train stops away."

"No kidding," he grinned.

"Hey," I suddenly had an idea, "how do your folks get up here?"

"By car," Pete shrugged. "Why?"

"My parents don't have a car. Maybe they could get together with your parents and form a car pool," I suggested. "You know—share expenses and everything."

"Sounds cool to me," he agreed. "It's a long

drive up here and my old lady would probably enjoy the company. I'll write them and see what they think."

"OK, I'll write my mom about it too . . ."

After that, my mother drove up with Pete's parents to visit me. The arrangement worked out fine for everybody concerned. Car pools were a common practice among the families of inmates who lived near each other.

For working, all of the convicts were paid a nickel a day, one dollar and fifty cents a month—standard prison wages. This sum was accredited to our accounts at the commissary (we never saw any cash) and purchases we made were then deducted. For the men who didn't have relations to send them additional funds, this money was just enough to buy a few packs of cigarettes each month. Whenever I wrote to my mother, I asked her to send me cash and she would usually enclose a five dollar bill in her next letter. That extra money made a great difference in the quality of life in prison. With it I could buy cans of food and milk to store in my cell locker and consume at leisure. It was a way of keeping sane.

Since my friend David had nobody on the outside to send him cash (his wife and parents wanted nothing to do with him) I would occasionally share my funds with him, sometimes buying him a couple of extra packs of cigarettes or aspirins, etc. Of course, I realized that it wasn't a smart idea to support a guy's habit, so I only did this once in awhile.

In the evenings around eight or nine o'clock, I

looked forward to preparing myself a snack with the goods I had purchased at the commissary. From my locker, I would take out a jar of mayonnaise, a can of tuna, and hot cherry peppers and proceed to make my favorite sandwich. I would stir all the ingredients into the can of tuna and then spread the gooey mixture onto the thick slices of bread we were allowed to take from the mess hall each evening. My mouth always watered as I was preparing this special treat; it was so delicious and spicy and reminded me of good Latin cooking. Often I made a couple of extra sandwiches for David.

Occasionally we had a relay system going on our tier. We passed sandwiches from cell to cell and every inmate would add an extra ingredient to each sandwich—like a group of hobos making a soup. At other times, one inmate would make up a pile of sandwiches in his cell and pass them down to his buddies.

"Hey, pass this on to cell five," he would inform the man in the next cell, and he in turn would hand it over to the inmate next to him and so on until the intended person would finally receive his sandwich. It seemed odd that this kind of sharing went on in prison.

A few cells down from mine, for example, there was a kind-hearted old Jew. Whenever he received a package from home, he would share all of its contents—mostly candy and matzoth crackers—with everybody on the tier. When he had food we were friendly to him, but when he didn't we avoided him. Out in the Big Yard nobody talked to him. He wasn't a "cool" person—the sort we would want to be seen associating with. For one thing, he was mentally unbalanced, and second, he stunk. He was one of those men—and there were plenty at Comstock —who didn't like to take a bath, and even in summer, when outside in temperatures over 90 degrees, he refused to take his coat off.

To wash my spicy sandwich down, I made myself a cup of coffee. Each evening, the water boy brought hot water to every inmate who asked for it, and to this I would add a teaspoon of commissary coffee. All of us had a cup of some sort from which to drink. I drank my coffee from an old mayonnaise jar which I had saved for expressly that purpose.

The sandwiches, the coffee, the sharing were the little things that made life in prison bearable.

One day in the carpentry shop Frank, a lanky Spaniard with straight black hair and squinty eyes, told me about his job. Every morning and afternoon he had to wait in the shop for Charlie, the civilian roofer, to arrive and then the two of them would walk to the town of Comstock to repair damaged roofs.

"It's a real good job, man," Frank said with obvious enthusiasm. "You get to go outside the walls and walk around and see the town. . . ."

"Man, I could use a change of scenery . . ." I sighed.

"Well, why don't you work with me?" Frank asked suddenly.

"Huh?" I was startled. "What do you mean?"

"Listen, the other guy who usually works with

Charlie and me is being turned loose soon. Why don't you apply for his job?" Frank suggested eagerly. "It's the best job around. You'll like it."

"Well, I dunno . . ." I hesitated, not wanting to get my hopes up. "I dunno nothin' about fixin' roofs."

"You don't need to," Frank assured me. "It's easy to learn. A cinch."

"Do you think I have a chance?" I asked him honestly.

"Sure. You're already working in the carpentry shop so you've got a better chance than anybody else," Frank advised me. "Hey, how much time you got left anyway?"

"Less than a year . . . why?"

"Good. Only the guys with a year or so left to serve get picked for this job. The authorities figure if you've only got a short time to go, you're not gonna try to escape and risk getting a few big ones slapped onto your sentence," Frank explained. "You can bet they don't let just anybody walk through those gates! Not on your life!"

"Guess not," I grinned.

"And Charlie's an OK guy," Frank added. "Kinda weird and old-fashioned, but you'll get along with him."

"OK, man, you've sold me," I laughed. "I'll apply for the job right away."

After being interviewed, I was accepted for the roofing job. Each morning, Frank and I would wait in the carpentry shop for Charlie and then we would set out on the day's rounds. Sometimes we stayed within the prison grounds, but more often than not, we journeyed into Comstock. Whenever we passed through those open front gates, my step picked up. Freedom was so close I could almost touch it.

"Wonder what it feels like to walk out of here for the last time?" I mused, a chill running up my spine at the very thought.

Even Charlie became livelier as we left the prison complex behind. In his thick Irish brogue, he cracked jokes to us and we grinned in spite of ourselves; his cheerfulness was infectious. Charlie was a jovial, good-natured fellow and his enthusiasm for life made him seem much younger than he was. Although he must have been in his late fifties, he was still in excellent physical condition—only his thinning gray hair and wrinkled weather-beaten face betrayed his age. He should have been thinking of retirement, but that was the farthest thing from his mind. He was just one of those men who enjoyed working, especially working outdoors.

As we walked along the road to the town of Comstock, Charlie would amuse us with interesting anecdotes about the community and point out the local sights.

"That's the warden's place over there," Charlie waved his hand. Looking in the direction he indicated, I could glimpse the warden's house—a mansion—half-hidden among the trees.

"And that's the old slate pit," Charlie informed us. "At one time, it used to supply all the slate needed for the roofs in the area, but it's abandoned now. . . ." The slate pit was a relic of Comstock's "hard-labor" days when the convicts were forced to hack away at the rock all day and then load the chunks of slate into trucks where they would be hauled away and later cut into square tiles. I was certainly glad those days were over.

Sometimes Charlie would talk to Frank and me about his children. We would just let him ramble on and on without really paying attention to what he was saying.

"Yes, sir, they're all married off now. Raisin' families of their own. I'm a grandfather, you know," he boasted proudly, "but I don't get to see my grandchildren very often—wee devils—because my kids are spread all across the country. A fine family . . . yes, siree, I'm mighty proud of the whole kit and kaboodle."

"Israel, are you married?" Charlie asked me once out of the blue.

"Nope."

"Guess you're a mite bit young," he reflected. "Got lots of time yet. But take my advice and find yourself a good wife. They're worth something."

"Yeah, sure," I humored him.

Sometimes if Charlie was in a really happy-go-lucky mood he would break into song:

"Oh, my darling, Oh, my darling, Oh, my darling Clementine . . ." or

"Waltzing Matilda, Waltzing Matilda . . ."

Charlie's voice was deep and rich and pleasant to listen to. I couldn't say as much for his selection of songs, though. They were crazy songs, songs that I had never heard before, "hillbilly" songs.

"C'mon, boys," he would urge Frank and me. "Sing along with me!"

"Uh-uh," I backed off. "No way, man."

"Yeah, we don't know the words," Frank added.

"Ah, sure'n they be simple. Listen. This one's my favorite: When Irish eyes are smilin', the whole world's bright and gay . . ."

When we didn't join in, Charlie would break off, "C'mon, boys. Sing! Sure'n you've got fine voices."

"Nah," I shrugged. "Not me."

Sometimes, forgetting himself, Charlie would stop in the middle of the road and dance a little jig. He looked so comical, Frank and I couldn't keep from laughing.

"Grab your partner round and round, Swing them to and all will frown. . . ."

I liked being with Charlie. His carefree, fun-loving spirit was a welcome change from the strict oppressive attitude of the other prison personnel. As the three of us strolled along that open road, surrounded by miles and miles of rolling countryside, I could almost forget that I was a prisoner—almost.

In the evenings, it was always hard to return again to my cell. . . .

After I had been working with Charlie and Frank for four months, Frank rushed over to me one morning all flushed with excitement.

"Man, it's happened!" he shouted. "It's finally happened."

"You being cut loose?" I asked, unable to keep the envy out of my voice.

"You bet, baby!"

"Lucky son-of-a-gun," I punched him in the forearm. "I wish it was me."

"Ah, you'll be next."

"Yeah, in another eight months . . ." I commented drily.

The day after Frank was released, I was very depressed. It felt strange to be working without him. I missed him. Charlie tried to cheer me up.

"Frank's gonna make it," he said. "Don't worry about him. He won't be back. And you're going to be out pretty soon too!" He opened his lunchbox and handed me an apple. "Here. This'll make you feel better." Charlie was always giving me something.

Three and a half months later the parole review committee visited Comstock. I was informed that I was to be one of the inmates called before them. It came as no great surprise to me—for the last month I had been aware that my turn for review was due and I had thought of nothing else.

The prison hummed with excitement. Everyone was speculating on who would be granted parole. It was expected that because the cell blocks were filled to capacity, a greater than average percentage of inmates would be released. In addition, the Thanksgiving and Christmas holidays were approaching and it was rumored that the committee was generally more lenient at this time of year. The odds seemed to be stacked in my favor.

As I waited for my turn to be interviewed, I tried not to get my hopes up too high. After all, I had been rejected once and I didn't want to suffer disappointment a second time. In my mind I ran over all the reasons why I should be granted parole: I had been careful not to get involved in many fights this past year, I had tried school again, and I had been trusted to work in the community. These points should count for something. But perhaps the most important reason was my change of attitude. It was hard to put a finger on exactly how or when I had changed, but now I *wanted* to get out of prison, I *wanted* to fit into society, I *wanted* to do something with my life!

Some of the inmates did not want to get out of prison. They actually enjoyed the prison routine and were content to let the authorities plan their life. In prison, they didn't have to worry about where the next meal was coming from or where to rest their head. They didn't have to worry about getting a job or paying the bills or disciplining the kids. They had a freedom in prison: a freedom from responsibility, a freedom from thinking and acting for themselves. But I definitely did not want to waste any more time behind bars. My only desire was to start living my own life again. That was a challenge I was ready to meet. . . .

The inmate ahead of me emerged from the examination room looking anything but pleased. He pushed by me, scowling darkly. Feeling like a new member about to be initiated into a gang, I walked through the open door and sat down on the familiar single chair facing the semicircle of five committee members.

One or two of the committee members glanced at me briefly, as if measuring my appearance against the records of my behavior—my progress report—spread out on the table before them.

"You seem to have been involved in numerous fights, Mr. Narvaez?" the only woman on the committee mused out loud, scanning the papers in front of her. She looked up suddenly.

"Yes, ma'am," I agreed politely. "If you don't want to be turned into a trick, you have to fight. . . ."

"I see." She nodded her head. She considered my explanation in silence. From her expression I could tell that she thought my reason was a satisfactory one. The others seemed to understand also.

"Your record shows that you've attended classes at the school here, Mr. Narvaez." The man sitting directly in front of me changed the line of questioning.

"Yes, sir, that's right."

"But," he continued, frowning, "it also shows that you failed to get your high school diploma. Why is that?"

"I dropped out," I answered bluntly.

"Why?" he persisted.

"I dunno," I said simply. "I just couldn't put my mind to that stuff."

He rubbed his chin reflectively.

"You don't need it, do you, to get out of here?" I asked anxiously, a sickening feeling beginning to creep all over me.

"No," he sighed. "It's not imperative, but—"

I didn't like the sound of that "but." "But what?" I wanted to shake him. "But what?" I kept silent.

"But it would certainly help you in the future. You should have stayed in school until you got it." He looked at me directly.

"Without a diploma, do you think you'll be able to get a job, Mr. Narvaez?" the bald man at the end of the table asked me.

"I don't see why not," I answered cockily.

They seemed impressed by my positive attitude.

"So you're confident that you could get one?"

"Sure."

"Have you a particular occupation in mind, Mr. Narvaez?" This from the lady.

"Well, ma'am, first of all I'm just gonna grab any old job that comes along," I said firmly.

"And after that? What then?" the balding man with the glasses eyed me shrewdly. "Do you have any long-range plans?"

"Oh, then I'm planning to go into the construction business. Carpentry."

"You like carpentry, eh?" the woman smiled.

"Uh-huh," I answered, but I was thinking that being able to fix broken stools didn't qualify me as a carpenter.

"How are you planning to get into that profession, Mr. Narvaez?" another member pursued the subject. "Is there a demand for carpenters now?"

"Well, sir, I hear that they're building a lot of houses out in California," I replied, remembering having read this in some newspaper. "They need carpenters badly."

One man nodded his head. "That's true. He's right. There's been a lot about the California housing boom in the news recently."

"Right," I continued. "That's where I plan on moving just as soon as I get enough cash to get out there. I don't want to live in New York anymore. I want to start life all over again. . . ."

I don't know why I said all of that. It just came off the top of my head. The truth was that I had made no plans. I had a vague idea that I would like to move out of New York and start out fresh in a new place. I don't know why I said California, but it proved to be a prophetic statement. One day I would indeed be moving to that state—but not under any circumstance I could ever have imagined beforehand. . . .

"Mr. Narvaez, you realize that even if we grant you parole, before you can be released, you must have a job lined up and waiting for you?" the man in front of me stated matter-of-factly.

"Yes, sir," I said. Word had spread among the inmates that this was one of the usual conditions of parole.

The parole board committee asked me a few more questions and then I returned to my cell. That night around midnight, a guard slipped an envelope through the bars—the envelope I had been anxiously waiting for. I picked it up with trembling hands and stared at my name scribbled across the front. At once both eager and reluctant to open it, I turned it over and over in my hands. That little envelope contained my fate.

Finally I could stand the suspense no longer. I tore the envelope open and pulled out the single sheet of paper. I unfolded it and read:

"PAROLE HAS BEEN GRANTED TO IS-RAEL NARVAEZ."

The paper fluttered to the floor. I jumped up and rattled the bars of my cell.

"Hey, guys, I made it! I'm getting out!" I let out an ecstatic whoop. Then I collapsed on my cot, shaking with laughter, and threw my pillow up in the air.

"I'm free! I'm free!" I punched the pillow. My joy knew no bounds.

I knew that before I could be given a release date, I had to get myself a job. But how do you go about finding a job when you're behind bars? I wrote my mother and she and my brothers visited local factories, but what could she say to the potential employers? "I've got a son who's coming from Alaska. Can you give him a job Monday?" Who's going to hire anybody that way?

"Man, I've got to find a job somehow," I poured out my misery to a fellow Puerto Rican, Bill, one afternoon as we walked around the Big Yard. I had originally met him on the handball courts and we had occasionally played together. I knew that he was intelligent and could perhaps solve my dilemma. "I've got to get out of this place! Right away. I don't want to spend another Thanksgiving here!"

Bill brooded over my problem in silence for a

few minutes. "Maybe I can help you," he said slowly.

"Yeah?" I asked eagerly. "How?"

"I can probably arrange a job for you—not a real job," he said hastily, "but I can get you a 'fix.'"

"What do you mean?" I asked, puzzled.

"Well, my mom has worked a long time—fifteen years—running a sewing machine in this garment factory, see? And she knows the manager real well," Bill explained. "Maybe she can work out a deal with this guy. . . . For fifty dollars he'll agree to let you fill out an application form and then say he's going to hire you. But then when you get out, he just won't have a job for you. You'll have to go and find a real one. See?"

"Yeah," I smiled. "That sounds like a pretty good idea to me. It may just work . . . ."

And it did. Job-fixing is a common practice among inmates.

On my last day of work, I was so excited as Charlie and I made the rounds, that I didn't pay attention to what was going on. I was lucky that I didn't fall off a roof! Charlie had to caution me more than once to watch what I was doing or I would be going home with a broken neck . . . .

Charlie said goodbye to me in the carpentry shop.

"Be good," he told me gruffly, trying to hide his emotion. "I don't want to see your mug around these parts again."

"Nah, you don't have to worry about that!" I said earnestly.

"Well, son, what are your plans now?"

"I'm goin' home to my family, I'm gonna get a job, and I'm gonna try my best not to come back here." I grinned.

"Good. Well, I wish you all the luck in the world." He shook my hand.

Saying goodbye to Chino was the hardest. We sat huddled together on the bleachers, talking quietly to one another.

"Take it easy," I told him hoarsely. After all we had been through together, a real bond of affection had developed between us. What could I say to him now? "Try not to get into trouble and you'll probably get out on parole too. . . ."

"Yeah," Chino smiled weakly. "By that time I'll be an old man."

"Listen," I tried to cheer him up, "when I get back to New York, I'm gonna get myself a job and I'm gonna send you some money so you can buy all the cigarettes and candy you want. OK?"

"OK," he said, staring at his feet. I had never seen him looking so sad.

"And if I run into your brother, I'll tell him you're doin' OK. . . ."

"Sure," he nodded, without looking at me.

There wasn't much else we could say to one another. One of us was going, one was staying behind. It was better to get it over with quickly.

"Catch you later," I said, slapping his palm. "I'll see you in the streets one of these days. . . ."

"Yeah, man, sure. . . ."

SEVENTEEN
Return to the World

On the final morning of my imprisonment, in October of 1963, the other men on my tier filed by my cell on their way to breakfast.

"Be seein' you."

"Take it easy, man."

"Stay out of trouble."

"Keep cool."

I listened to their footsteps echo hollowly on the wooden planks of the catwalk, and then I was left alone in silence. I surveyed my naked cell, that ten-by-six-foot cage that I had called home for the past two years. Every trace of my occupancy had vanished.

The day before, knowing that I would have no need for them on the outside, and also not wishing to take any prison souvenirs with me, I had given away all my personal belongings. Chino had inherited my most prized possessions: my rugs, my fancy toilet covering, and my last cans of food and candy. Although I had been forced to turn in my prison denims to the authorities, I had passed along my underwear to grateful men on my tier, men who had no relatives to send them such necessities—luxuries in this place.

A guard came for me shortly after seven o'clock. My cell door clicked open electronically. I jumped to my feet and stepped through it for the last time. When they returned from breakfast, my fellow inmates would find an empty cell. The prison authorities planned all departures this way—it was easier on those who had to stay behind.

The "hack" escorted me to a small room on the ground level. "I'll wait outside while you change. Don't be long, huh," he instructed me and shut the door.

A cheap civilian suit lay hanging over the back of a chair, the sole piece of furniture in the room. Earlier in the week, the prison tailor had dug up this second-hand suit and had roughly altered it to my measurements. I held the jacket at arm's length.

"I wonder what poor dead dummy he pinched this rag off of?" I grunted in disgust. "Well, beggars can't be choosers. . . ." Anything was better than regulation shirts and dungarees.

I stripped, casting my denims in a heap on the floor, and struggled into the suit. The jacket stretched tight around my chest. In recent years I had broadened out across the shoulders, gained weight and muscle. Critically, I inspected my mirror image.

"Man, this sure ain't my style," I groaned,

thinking that I looked like an immigrant fresh off the boat. "If the MauMaus could only see me now. . . ." The outfit was a far cry from the sharp leather jacket I had sported as a gang leader. Of course, those days were far behind me now. I had no desire to return to gang life. That was kid's stuff. And I was no longer a cocky kid; I was a man. I was twenty-one-and-a-half years old. Bitterness, like an overflowing sewer, surged up within me. I had been cheated of my youth. The best five years of my life had been wasted in this dunghole. Nobody could give them back.

"Man, I've got a lotta catchin' up to do," I muttered. "Movies . . . gigs . . . chicks." I had to make up for lost time. Begin living again.

I followed the "hack" to the warden's office. The warden handed me several sheets of paper—my release forms—and I signed them all without reading them. The faster the formalities were over with, the faster I could get out of this joint. When I had scrawled my signature across the last one, the warden lit up his pipe and smiled at me coldly.

"As you know, Mr. Narvaez," the warden said, chewing on the stem of his pipe, "technically you have four months remaining to serve of your sentence. For that time period, you are required by law to report to your parole officer once every two weeks. Make sure that you don't miss any visits. It's very important. We don't want you back here. . . ."

I nodded solemnly, "Right."

"Now this is your one-way train ticket to New York." He pushed the ticket across his desk. I picked it up and stared at it. Never had I seen anything so beautiful! A one-way ticket out of hell. "And this," the warden handed me a crisp ten dollar bill, "should be enough to cover any minor expenses such as your meals and cab fare or whatever."

I folded the bill neatly in half. "Thanks," I said grudgingly, but I was thinking, "Ten bucks. Ten lousy bucks—All I have to show for the five best years of my life." I stuffed it into my suit pocket.

"Well," the warden rose from his chair behind the desk. He shook my hand, "Good luck, Mr. Narvaez. I hope we never see you in Great Meadows again."

"No, sir. Not me. I'll never be within a hundred miles of here."

Although I was determined never to see the inside of a prison again, God had other plans for my life.

Another "hack" escorted me across the deserted courtyard to the main gates. We walked in silence. An early morning rain had washed the pavement; I sidestepped the puddles. The October air was damp and chilly, the sky bleak and gray, but for all I cared it could have been hailing brass knuckles.

I held my breath as the gates swung open. Only a person who has been robbed of his freedom understands what I felt at that moment . . .

"Wait a minute." The guard stopped me. "I have something for you." He handed me a small bundle.

"What's this?" I asked, puzzled.

"Your mail for the last five years. Only letters from your immediate family were passed on to you. Prison regulations."

I wanted to tell him just what he could do with his stupid prison regulations! "Lot of good they're gonna do me now . . ." I remarked sarcastically.

He led me through the open gates. "See that flag?" he said, pointing to a red flag hanging on a pole beside the railway tracks.

"Yeah?"

"When the train comes around that bend, you'd better grab that flag fast and start waving it. Because if you don't the train won't stop. And if you miss it, buddy, you can't come back inside."

As if I would want to! "Listen, man," I informed the guard, "wild horses couldn't drag me back inside those gates. I'd sleep out here in the pouring rain if I had to. . . ."

I had no intention, however, of missing that train. I walked over to the bench beside the tracks where two other ex-convicts were already patiently waiting. I nodded to them and sat down.

"Smoke?" The one on my right offered me a cigarette.

I shook my head.

"Where you goin'?" he asked me. "New York?"

"Yeah."

"Me too. Manhattan," he said conversationally.

"Boy, it's sure gonna be swell to see my old lady. If she hasn't run out on me again, that is," he added, scowling. "You married?"

"Nah."

"Smart. Got a job?"

"Nope, not yet."

"Me neither. It ain't so bad for me though. . . . I can live off my old lady. She makes good money," he chuckled. "Well, I hope you make it, man."

"Yeah. . . ."

After that brief exchange, we lapsed into a companionable silence. Before long the fine mist turned into a drizzle. Rain dripped off the curl on my forehead, running down my nose and onto the bundle of letters on my lap. I had forgotten all about them. Casually I leafed through the bundle, noticing that most of the letters were from friends and relatives. One, I observed ruefully, was from Anna, the girl I had been going with before my arrest. My mother had written that she had married a few years ago and already had a couple of kids. Suddenly I had a great urge to hold a girl, any girl, to hold her close and smell her perfume and kiss her soft lips. Man, I had missed a lot!

A photograph of two young boys caught my eye. Shocked, I recognized that one boy was Nicky, and the other me! It had been taken over five years ago, on the day we had given our testimonies at the tent meeting in Elmira. The photograph had been reprinted on one side of a tract; the reverse side had a gospel message. I crumbled it up in my hand. Then I noticed the

letters from David Wilkerson. Suddenly an un-
bidden, unwanted image of the skinny preacher
with the cornsilk hair, pointing his bony finger at
me, flashed through my mind. "Jesus loves you,"
he had said.

Angrily I sprang to my feet, trying to shake
off the memory. As far as I was concerned,
Nicky was dead, the preacher was dead, everyone was dead. I walked over to the ditch beside
the railway tracks. Beneath me, a few soggy,
mud-smeared envelopes were scattered in the
weeds and bushes. I tossed my bundle of un-
opened letters into the ditch to join the others.

Many years later I discovered that David Wilkerson, upon hearing of my imprisonment in the
late spring of 1959, had immediately tried to
write me and send correspondence courses
through the prison chaplain. Of course, because I
had been allowed to receive mail only from my
immediate family, his letters never reached me
until the day of my release. I do not know why I
never received the courses, but the fact that I
was officially registered as a Catholic in prison
files may have had something to do with it.

Twenty minutes later, though every minute
had seemed like an hour, the long blast of a train
horn broke the silence. Madly, all three of us
scrambled to the pole. I reached it first and
tore the flag down, waving it over my head
frantically.

The train thundered around the bend and
screeched to a halt a few hundred feet past us.
We ran to the last car, slipping in the mud and

stumbling in the shale siding. As he reached the car, the same man who had offered me a cigarette cried out excitedly.

"Hope you find a job, man. Good luck!"

"Yeah, you too. Keep cool." I swung up onto the steps behind him.

"Ticket, please." The conductor took my ticket and punched it without looking up to meet my eyes. I felt humiliated. Of course, he knew what I was. . . . The high prison walls were plainly in view behind me, stark against the gray sky, the only building for miles around. As I made my way to the back of the coach, I could feel all eyes riveted upon me, upon my shabby, ill-fitting suit and mud-splattered shoes.

Feeling like a cockroach scuttling down a drainpipe, I slid into the empty seat at the back of the car. Crouching as far as I could into the corner, I pressed my burning face against the cold pane of the window and shut out the rest of the world.

For the first time I felt a twinge of fear. I had experienced my first contact with normal society and it had not been pleasant. "Will I be able to make it on the outside?" I seriously questioned myself, but then after awhile I brushed away the doubts. "After what I've been through, I could survive anything. I'll make it, all right."

I settled back into my seat and began to enjoy the ride. All afternoon the train snaked through the mountains, stopping at every town along the way. I watched the passing scenery, but I wasn't really seeing any of it. My thoughts always drifted to my family and the coming reunion. . . .

Late in the evening the train pulled into Grand Central Station. I hurried down the aisle and out onto the platform. The crowd jostled me along. In front of me a young man swung his girl up into his arms and embraced her. Nobody had come to meet me, but then nobody knew that I would be here. I wanted my arrival to be a surprise.

In front of the station, I hailed a taxicab.

"Where do you want to go, mac?" The driver eyed me in his mirror. His thick Brooklyn accent made me feel right at home.

In awe, I repeated his question to myself, "Where do I want to go? Somebody's actually asking ME where I want to go?" After so many years of taking orders, it was hard to believe that I had a choice. I could go anywhere. . . .

I gave him the address of my parents' place in the Bronx, the one that I had memorized from my mother's letters.

"OK, man." The driver set the meter and we were off.

As we darted in and out of traffic, I tried to tell him the fastest way to get there.

"Listen, mac," he interrupted me in mid-sentence. "I'm doing the driving, OK? I'm taking a short-cut. I'll go your way if you want, but it's the long way."

"Well, I haven't been in New York for awhile. . . ."

"That's right. Everything's changed, man. I'm taking the shortest route I know."

I left the driving to him and relaxed against the seat, content to watch the neon signs, the theater

marquees, the fruit stands, and the all-night dives
flash by. As we crossed the Harlem River, I
rolled down the window to let the cool air wash
over my face.

The cab pulled to the curb in front of a sooty
blackstone tenement building. "This is the place,
mac."

The number beside the door checked with the
one I had memorized. My parents had only
moved here recently. I knew the neighborhood
well, however, because when we had first come
to America, we had lived in the basement of my
grandparents' tenement building, only a few
blocks away.

"How much do I owe you?" I asked, reaching
for the ten dollar bill in my pocket. After tipping
him, I had only a handful of change left.

I ran up the steps in front of the building.
Inside, I stopped on the landing for a moment to
smooth down my hair and straighten my suit.
Everything was quiet. It was well after midnight.

I climbed the flight of stairs to the second floor
and found the number I was looking for. I hesitated for a fraction of a second and then knocked
on the door. I waited. Nobody answered. I
knocked again, louder. This time I heard footsteps, then the telltale scratching of the peephole,
and finally, the sliding of the safety chain across
its latch.

My kid brother Johnny opened the door. We
stared dumbly at each other. I hardly recognized
him; he had grown a foot taller and his
shoulder-length hair made him look like a girl. I
didn't realize it then, but I had come face-to-face

with a strange social phenomenon—Beatlemania. With my own hair cropped short, prison style, we made an incongruous pair.

"Israel, is that you?" Johnny threw his arms around me in a tight bearhug. That felt strange; in prison, men didn't touch each other. I hadn't had physical contact with another human being, unless it was my fist connecting with a jaw, for five years.

"How you doin', bro?" I punched him on the shoulder affectionately. "Give me five." We slapped each other's palms.

"Man, is it good to see you!" Johnny grinned from ear to ear. "C'mon in. Don't stand out there all night."

I followed him into the living room. The apartment, as always, smelled of good Puerto Rican cooking. Suddenly I remembered how hungry I was. My last meal had been breakfast.

"Oh, man, is there anything around to eat? I'm starving . . . ." I craved one of my mother's home-cooked meals. No more mess-hall slop for me!

"Nah. If Mom woulda known. . . ."

"Never mind. I'll help myself later. But where is she?" I demanded eagerly. "Where's Mom?"

"In the back room. Asleep."

I walked down the short hall to the end room, passing a Saint Mary hanging on the wall with two candles burning in front of it. My mother had lit a candle for me faithfully every night. "Much good they've done me . . ." I muttered, but though I wouldn't admit it, the gesture had touched me deeply.

I pushed the door open quietly and tiptoed over to the bed. My mother was curled up under the covers, looking much like a small balloon. For a moment I stood above her, listening to her heavy, steady breathing, and then I bent over and gently shook her shoulders.

"Mom . . . Mom . . . wake up . . ." I whispered in her ear. "It's me, Israel. I'm back." She didn't stir. I shook her a little harder.

"Wha—" she opened her eyes and stared blankly at me for a few seconds. Then she realized who I was.

"Israel!" She threw back the blankets and stumbled out of bed toward me. I enfolded her warm, round body in my arms. We hugged and kissed each other. I felt her body tremble and held her away from me.

"Mom, what's wrong . . . ?"

"Aw, you know me. Always weeping." With the back of her hand she tried to brush away the tears streaming down her cheeks. It was a losing battle. My mother gushed out tears like a Brooklyn fire hydrant on a hot July day. She fumbled in her housecoat pocket for a tissue.

"Here." I handed her a fresh one from the dresser. She dabbed at the corners of her eyes.

"Why didn't you tell me you were coming home?" she reproached me. "I'd have made a big dinner for you and—"

I put my arm around her shoulder. "I wanted to surprise you. Besides, I didn't want you to make a big fuss." I looked fondly at her tear-stained face, and then examined it more closely. Something was wrong—my mother had changed.

Then I knew what it was. She had grown old. For the first time, I noticed the gray strands of hair at her temples, the sagging cheeks, the dark shadows beneath her eyes. Deep wrinkles furrowed her forehead, carved from years of fear and pain. I looked at her weary face and died inside. With a stab of guilt, I realized that I had done that to her—I was the cause of her suffering. And I suddenly knew, too, how much my mother loved me. Then, from out of nowhere, a vision of Christ nailed to the cross sprang to my mind.

"Mom," I half sobbed, holding her very tight. "Mom, I love you." I choked the words out. It was the first time I had ever told her. "And I'm sorry for what I've done. Forgive me." I had never asked anybody to forgive me before. What was happening to me?

"Israel, my son. You're home now. That's all that matters."

"Don't worry about me anymore, Mom. I've changed. I'm gonna get a good job and everything's gonna be all right. You'll see." Somehow, I vowed to myself, I'll pay her back for all that she's been through because of me.

She squeezed my arm. "You want me to fix you a sandwich, huh?"

"No, I'm OK. You go back to bed."

I closed the door behind me softly. In the living room my brother was sprawled out on the couch, drinking beer. He held the bottle up. "You want some? There's a couple of bottles in the fridge."

"Nah." I shook my head and sat down beside

him. We rapped for awhile and then I went to bed. As I drifted off to sleep, I thought of how wonderful it was going to be to wake up to a curtained window, and toast and coffee at a kitchen table.

I had been set free from one prison. I had yet to be set free from the dark prison of my soul.

EIGHTEEN
"Nobody Hires an Ex-con"

When I was released from prison, I had reached the breaking point. I knew that I couldn't take any more years—even months—behind bars. For this reason, I was determined to try my best to make it in society.

It helped to know that my family was behind me—especially my mother. A lot of men come out of prison only to discover that they have been deserted by their spouses and rejected by their families. They are left to struggle through those first difficult months alone. Nobody cares what happens to them—whether they make it or not—and they have nothing to live for. In their extreme loneliness, they are often driven to commit crimes which eventually send them back to prison—where they at least have companionship.

In my case, however, I realized that even if I didn't care what happened to me, my mother did, and this strongly influenced my desire to go straight. I had seen the effect my years behind bars had wrought on her and I did not want to hurt her in this way again. To make something of my life became a great challenge to me.

"Maybe I *can* be somebody," I thought. "Maybe I *can* come out on top." I wanted to prove to my family that I, the underdog, could make it.

Fortunately, too, I had come through my prison years with all my mental faculties intact. While serving my sentence, I had *not* gone insane, I had *not* been attacked, I had *not* been raped. I had suffered few permanent emotional scars. For this I praise God. Although at the time, I wouldn't acknowledge him, he had indeed kept a guiding hand on the affairs of my life.

If we believe not, yet he abideth faithful: he cannot deny himself (2 Timothy 2:13).

I realized that if I was to succeed, if I was to stay out on the streets, I had to get myself a job. A job would provide me with stability, security, a sense of accomplishment and acceptance by society. Unlike many other ex-cons, I was willing to start at the bottom and try anything. I desperately wanted a job—any job.

The day after my release from prison, I dutifully reported to my parole officer, making my first visit of many. Once in every two weeks for the next four months I had to report to him so that he could follow my progress.

"What happened to the job you were supposed

to have lined up, Mr. Narvaez?" the parole officer asked me, after he found out I was not employed.

"It fell through . . ." I lied.

"That's too bad," the parole officer remarked sympathetically. "But you must find yourself a job within two weeks. If you fail to, I'm afraid that it will be considered violation of parole. . . ."

I knew what that meant—in all probability I would be sent back to prison to complete my sentence!

"If you can't find employment on your own, Mr. Narvaez," he went so far as to say, "I'll see what I can do to help you."

"Thanks," I mumbled appreciatively. I wasn't sure whether this was just a line or not. At any rate, I knew I had to get a job or else . . . and I didn't want to even think of the "or else"!

My father advised me not to waste any time looking for a job on my own but to go to an employment agency immediately. I followed his advice and forked out one hundred dollars to an agency in Manhattan, which in return guaranteed me a job.

At the agency, when I filled out the application form, I lied about my past. Who wanted to hire an ex-con? I found it difficult to cover up the five long years that I had wasted in prison. It required all my ingenuity to invent plausible excuses for the gap in my life.

The man who examined my form may have realized that I was lying through my teeth, but he didn't try to trip me up. Instead, he briefly scanned my answers, asked a few more general questions, and then made some phone calls. I got the distinct impression that all he was concerned about was finding me a job—any job—because the sooner he found me one, the sooner he could collect his fee.

I thought, "It shouldn't be hard for him to locate me a factory job." From what I had heard, it wouldn't have surprised me if he had some kind of racket going on with the factory employers—many of whom had a suspicious habit of letting the men they hired go after only six months.

He arranged some appointments for interviews for me and I left his office. That afternoon, I went to my first interview. I was nervous. Everything was going along smoothly until my potential employer pulled a fast one:

"Why didn't you serve a term in the military?" He gazed at me with penetrating eyes.

I didn't know how to answer him! Caught by surprise, I blurted out the truth: "Well, sir, I'm, uh, fresh out of prison. . . ."

My potential employer looked visibly shocked. "Oh. I see. Yes, well, we'll take your application into consideration and contact you if you get the job. . . ."

The interview ended abruptly. I walked out. From the man's expression, there was no way in the world that I was going to get that job.

"Nobody wants to take a chance on an ex-con," I muttered bitterly.

That night, I discussed the interview with my younger brother Albert.

"If anybody asks you again why you weren't in the armed services," my more worldly wise brother advised me, "just say you're 4F."

I was puzzled. "What does 4F mean?"

"It means," he explained to me patiently, "that you've got something physically wrong with you. A handicap. Then, if they ask you what, just say you've got flat feet. The army doesn't take people with flat feet."

I looked at my brother, still not understanding what he had said. "Why don't they take people with flat feet? What's the difference?"

"People with flat feet get tired too quickly. They can't walk very far."

"Oh. OK." I was a little ashamed of my ignorance.

During my next interview, if the question of military service arose, I answered as my brother had suggested. Some of the interviewers swallowed my excuses and some didn't. It was easy to trap me. Five years of one's life are tremendously difficult to explain away in a believable manner.

Usually the interviews ended with a "Don't call us, we'll call you" line. I knew of course that as soon as I walked out of that office, my application form would be thrown into the nearest garbage can. Sometimes I felt like I had invisible cell bars all around me—but this only made me want to fight all the harder to break free.

One day, when I was feeling particularly discouraged, I went for an interview the agency had arranged for me at a lamp factory. The factory was only a few blocks away from where I lived.

"Man, it sure would be nice if I could make this walk every morning," I thought to myself whimsically. Of course, I shouldn't even have been thinking that because, as usual, I was probably going to be turned down. There was no sense in getting my hopes up.

The manager seemed to like me at first sight. He took me on a tour of the factory and showed me the room where I would be working if I was hired. He didn't ask me any awkward questions at all. He swallowed my story, hook, line, and sinker.

"Are you mechanically inclined?" the manager asked me, after explaining that the job involved assembling lamps.

I didn't have anything to lose. "Sure," I told him confidently, "I've fixed dozens of things at one time or another." I looked at the lamps he pointed out to me, and it didn't appear that a lot of brains were required to put them together.

"Do you think you can handle the job?"

I stared at him, not believing what I had heard. "Easy."

"OK," he smiled at me. "You can start Monday."

I reported for work on Monday, eager to begin. The lamp factory specialized in antique lamp kits. I was given a detailed diagram of a finished lamp, which had all the various parts numbered and indicated the order in which these parts were to be assembled. The parts were all kept in individual bins beside my working bench. I tackled my first lamp, following the step-by-step instructions on the diagram. When I finished, I plugged it in and the light bulb came on—the lamp was a success.

In the days that followed, however, I made my share of goofs. Sometimes the light bulb refused to come on. When this happened, the foreman would come along and point out the problem, which usually involved crossed wires. He was a nice guy and didn't get annoyed with me. He only shrugged, "Everybody makes mistakes."

The lamp factory was a small one and employed about twenty people. Some of my co-workers were Puerto Rican and they were very friendly to me. Often as we worked, they would discuss their personal problems with me. They were so wrapped up in their own lives, that they didn't notice that I never talked about mine. That was a good thing. It meant that I didn't have to lie. I never volunteered any information about myself; I kept my mouth shut. Even after I had worked there for a couple of months and my work was judged to be satisfactory, I knew that if the boss ever found out that I was an ex-con, I was in danger of losing my job.

Hiding my past became almost a game to me. It was always as though I had something over everybody else—my own private joke.

On weekends, my brother John and I would buy packs of beer. Sometimes we would stay at home and drink it, but more often than not, John would invite me to come with him to the candy store on Longfellow Avenue. That's where his friends hung out, and so, he was quick to inform me, did a lot of pretty girls. I didn't need much persuading. We walked the five blocks to the candy store, drinking the beer in a paper bag as we went along, finishing it before we arrived.

Inside the candy store, we stood around listening to the Spanish rock songs that blared from the juke box. We lived in a predominantly Puerto Rican area and most of the kids in the neighborhood had grown up with a taste for the Latin beat.

John had been right. A lot of pretty girls were hanging around the candy store, but they were much too young for me. After all, I was a grown-up workingman now, almost twenty-two. That's not to say that I didn't enjoy talking to the girls, because I did. It had been so long.

Girls, I soon discovered, had changed a lot. The Beatles had produced a new generation of female. They spoke differently, they dressed differently, and they acted differently. They even thought differently. We had nothing in common. I couldn't sweet-talk them like I used to or play the same old love game. They were swallowing none of my old lines.

The guys the girls were attracted to wore patched-up blue jeans and grew their hair down to their shoulders. I wore tight slacks and pointed shoes, and kept my hair cropped close to my scalp, prison style. I was still stuck in the mold of the late 1950s; the early sixties had completely passed me by. It was ironic that once the way I looked would have been considered "cool," but now it was "square." I felt bewildered by all the changes that had taken place in society in five years. Sometimes I felt like a real misfit.

I found it hard to really talk with anybody.

John never told his friends that I was an ex-con, and though they themselves never asked me about the past, I could sense their unspoken questions.

After a few months, John introduced me to his friend Vic and the two of us hit it off right from the beginning. We started to go out to clubs together and drink. Vic introduced me to some girls who were closer to my own age and we double-dated. Little did I know that one of these girls was to be my future wife. . . .

Sometimes at night, as I lay on my bed drifting off to sleep, I would imagine that cell bars surrounded me in that dark room. Then I would hear the sound of the water boy coming, hear his can squeaking back and forth and water pouring. . . . Frequently I had nightmares about being back in prison again, and I would wake up shaking. It took me many years to get over these bad memories.

After sticking it out at the lamp factory for about a year, I decided to change jobs. I began working at a factory that manufactured steel doors, washing the doors down with chemicals which removed the oil from the surface and made it possible to paint the steel. Even though I wore an asphalt bib while I was washing the doors, I still managed to get filthy from all the paint, chemicals, and sawdust scattered around. The smell was overpowering and it stayed with me wherever I went all day. In the evening when I left the factory, I carried it home with me. I hated it. I was forever taking showers to get rid of that awful smell that clung to me. I didn't like this job, but I stuck to it because the pay was good.

Later, I worked as a delivery boy for a busy coffee shop in Manhattan. The coffee shop was famous for its sandwiches and did a good business. At noon, the phone would ring constantly with lunch orders.

As a delivery boy, I would grab the lunch packets and hurry them over to the customers in the surrounding office buildings. At first I just dashed into the posh lobbies of these buildings, expecting to take the elevator up. The elevator operators, however, had a different idea. Eying my casual dress of shirt and slacks and the lunch bags I carried, they gave me a dirty look and refused to allow me onto their elevator. I wasn't good enough to mix with their clientele. Instead, I had to go around to the back entrance and take the slower freight elevator. By the time I got to the floors I wanted, my hot lunches would be cold. The name of the game was speed: the faster I delivered, the happier the customer and the higher the tip. Since increasing my tips was my main objective, I tried to figure out a way to save time.

One day I got the bright idea of disguising myself as a businessman, so I got all dressed up in a fancy suit and hid the lunch bags in a brown leather briefcase. I walked through the lobbies and onto the elevators with as much dignity as I could, and though the operators sometimes eyed me with suspicion, I was always whisked to the floors I wanted. My plan worked like a charm: I doubled my tips. "You have to use your head if you want to get anywhere in this world," I said to myself, and meant to do just that.

As I hustled after the bucks, the owner of the coffee shop, a nice Jewish man, began to notice that I was making more deliveries than the other boys. From experience he knew which of his customers were the big tippers, and he started to give me all their orders. I rushed the lunches over as fast as I could, always slowing to a more dignified pace as I entered the lobbies of the office buildings. I was usually rewarded with fifty cents for my trouble by the big spenders, a dime or a quarter by the more stingy ones.

Another trick of the trade I learned was to bribe the elevator operators. To butter them up, I brought them free lunches. They really went for that. From then on, even if the elevators were crowded to capacity, they always managed to squeeze me on somehow.

Whenever I stepped off the elevator at the floor I wanted, I always felt like I was entering another world. The various accounting, business, law, and advertising firms had such grand executive suites, that I was quite in awe of my plush surroundings. Never had I imagined that people worked in the middle of such luxury. "Man," I thought to myself with a certain envy, "it sure would be nice to work where some of these guys work."

My business suit didn't fool these men. Even though they joked around with me, I was always aware that they thought of me as "just a delivery boy." Some of them would say, "Here," and flip me a quarter, in the same manner as they might tell a dog, "Sit," and toss him a bone.

They made me want to show them that I could make it too. They gave me a taste of the good life and I wanted it for myself. I began to dream of one day having my own office and my own desk with my name plate. "Money talks, if nothing else," I thought grimly.

I got a chance to handle some of this money sooner than I had expected. The owner of the coffee shop and I were getting along very well together. One day he asked me to run over to the bank and get change for the day's business. He put several hundred dollars in my hand—more cash than I had ever seen at once in my entire life. I walked across the street to the Chase-Manhattan Bank, marveling all the while in his trust. I could have walked out the front door and never looked back—but I didn't. After that the trip to the bank became a routine part of my job and the trust between the owner and me grew.

The owner rewarded me with all kinds of thoughtful favors. For instance, while the other delivery boys were allowed to take only certain kinds of sandwiches for their own lunch, I had the whole range to choose from. Usually I snapped up the pastrami or the turkey ones. At the end of the day, whenever there was any pastry left over, the owner always winked at me and told the waitress: "Give it to Israel. He's OK."

Directly across the street from my parents' apartment, where I still lived, was a storefront Pentecostal church. Twice during the week and sometimes on Sunday, a loudspeaker blasted out a recording of Nicky Cruz giving his testimony. Every now and then I was horrified to hear him mention my name. This recording was really beginning to get on my nerves—over and over it played until I wanted to scream!

My mother didn't like it either. It brought back bad memories for both of us. She wanted me to march over to that church and order the minister to stop playing that record at once. In my mind, I rehearsed just what I would say to that minister:

"I don't want to hear any more of that jive. Cool it, man. If you want to play that nonsense, play it to the church people!"

Somehow I never found the courage to confront him. . . .

Of course, today I realize that a church right across the street from where I lived, playing a recording with my own name on it, was not the amazing coincidence that I had first thought it to be. Clearly, the Lord was using that recording of Nicky's testimony to speak to me. Unfortunately, I wasn't listening—yet.

NINETEEN
Rosa

"Hey, Israel," my buddy Vic said to me one Friday evening in 1965, as we walked together over to the dance hall. "Have I got a chick lined up for you!"

"Yeah?" I replied without much enthusiasm. I had been a victim of Vic's taste in women before.

"You bet. Wait until you see her. She's outa sight!"

"Lucky me. When do we meet?"

"Tonight," Vic said matter-of-factly. "At the dance hall. They're coming at eight o'clock. It's all arranged. Last week I met this groovy chick Elba who just happened to have an older sister, and she's bringing her along tonight."

"Yeah," I said drily. "My blind date. She better be good, Vic, or I'm gonna slit your throat."

"Don't worry. You can trust old Vic."

As it turned out, I need not have worried.

Elba's sister and I hit it off right from the beginning. Rosa was a sweet Puerto Rican girl, with long dark hair, small green eyes, and a warm smile. She was shy with me at first, which only added to her attractiveness, but as the evening wore on, I discovered that she had a very pleasant personality. We talked easily and naturally with one another—I found that I was really enjoying her company. We danced and talked and danced some more. We danced very well together.

Near the end of the evening, when we had decided to sit out a dance and had the table all to ourselves, Rosa began to talk to me very seriously. Up to this point, we had been exchanging trivialities in a light, joking banter. I had found out, for example, that she had only been living in New York City for about five years. Now Rosa thought it was time to explain her personal affairs.

"I'm divorced," Rosa told me quietly. "And I've got three small children."

I digested this information in silence.

"I left my husband," she went on to explain, "because he beat me. He used to drink a lot. . . . When he was drunk, he turned into a brute." She told me some of the things he used to do in a drunken rage.

I sympathized with her. "What kind of man would do those things?" I wondered angrily. "Especially with three little kids in the house?" Of course, having grown up on the streets of Brooklyn, I had seen and heard it all before.

"I stayed with him for the children's sake,"

Rosa sighed. "But then, one day, I just couldn't take it anymore. I walked out on him, taking the children with me. I moved into my sister's place—I had nowhere else to go. . . ."

"Yeah, I know how it is," I told her. I appreciated her honesty. Her past life didn't matter to me—I was only interested in the present.

I did not tell Rosa very much about myself. She had given me the perfect opportunity to share with her about my past, but I let it go by. I guess I lacked the courage. I was afraid of scaring her away—who wanted to date an ex-con?

After that, Rosa and I began to see each other quite regularly. Our courting did not always come off as smoothly as I would have liked. . . .

On one of our first dates together, I walked over to her sister's apartment to pick her up. I was all dressed up in my best suit, a brand new, shiny gray sharkskin, which had cost me quite a bundle. I decided the effect was worth it.

Recently, I had started taking singing lessons, still cherishing the old dream of making it to the top, and I had bought this suit especially to wear to practices at the studio. Not long ago, the studio had arranged a public appearance for its students at Carnegie Hall, so that we could get experience in front of an audience. For my singing debut, dressed in a tuxedo, I had chosen "I Believe." "I believe for every drop of rain that falls, a flower grows. . . ."

Now as I walked along, I was conscious of my smart image reflected in the store windows. I was going all out to impress Rosa and I was confident that I would succeed.

Rosa looked genuinely happy to see me and invited me into the apartment to wait. She wasn't quite ready to go. I sat down on the sofa and she offered me a drink. I chose Puerto Rican rum— although afterward I wished I had chosen water. When she brought my drink over to me, I guess she was a little nervous, because as she went to hand me the glass, it slipped out of her hand, and the rum and ice cubes spilled all over me. I looked down at the nasty dark brown stain slowly spreading over my brand new suit and could have cried.

Rosa gasped and ran to get a washcloth. She dabbed at the stain but it was no use. My suit was ruined forever. Rosa apologized over and over again. I brushed her apologies off with a, "Oh, it's nothing. I can always buy another suit." For me to say that, I must have liked her an awful lot.

For as long as I have had the privilege of knowing Rosa, she has been making that kind of bungle. It's part of her charm!

Sometimes I wonder how our courtship ever got off the ground. Shortly after this incident, Vic and Elba, Rosa and I were all returning to the girls' apartment after a night out on the town. They invited us in for a cup of coffee, but before long, naturally, we were smooching. Vic and Elba had made themselves comfortable on one side of the living room while Rosa and I had claimed the other side. We were all so absorbed in what we were doing, that it took us all a couple of minutes to realize that someone was knocking on the door, quite insistently. It couldn't be anyone else but Louisa, the youngest sister, the serious working sister who paid the rent. Vic stole to the door and looked through the peephole, just to make sure. It was Louisa, all right.

Vic and I bid the girls a hasty goodbye. We didn't want Louisa to catch us in her apartment at so late an hour—it was almost midnight. It might give her the wrong impression of us.

We crawled out of the back window onto the fire escape and from there jumped down into the alley. Luckily the apartment was on the first floor and we didn't have far to jump. Now that we were safe, Vic and I just walked away into the night, laughing.

Rosa and I continued to see a lot of each other that year. Mostly, we went drinking and dancing and to the movies together. I was becoming quite fond of her. She was different from the other girls I had known. We were able to talk about a lot of things. We understood each other—we had both been through hell. Even though she was a year older than I, I thought that she cooked - pretty good and that she kept her children clean, and that she would make a good wife. I broached the subject of marriage.

"How would you like to marry me?" I asked her bluntly one night, as we were sitting on the sofa together. I had one arm draped casually around her shoulder. My question had come out of the blue and I thought it would surprise her. It didn't.

"Sure. Why not?" She looked up at me with a teasing expression on her lovely face.

I thought she thought I was joking. "Listen, Rosa," I said very solemnly, watching her face closely, "I'm for real now."

She didn't smile. "Me too," she said so quietly I hardly caught the words.

And so, in the month of May, 1966, in a civil ceremony officiated by a justice of the peace, Rosa and I became man and wife. Vic and Elba were our only witnesses.

When I first met Rosa, I had been working as a delivery boy for the Manhattan restaurant. When I began to consider marriage, however, I decided to get a better job. I visited another employment agency and they lined up an interview for me with a stocks and bonds company on Wall Street that was desperate for trainees. The prospects sounded good, so off I went.

When I arrived, I was given an examination that involved matching names and numbers. My exam papers were marked, and then I was called in for an interview. The manager asked me about my educational background.

"I went to the University of Puerto Rico," I lied, not even knowing whether such a university really existed. I was reluctant to say I had just quit a job as a delivery boy.

"Oh, that's very good," he was smiling. He ruffled through the papers on his desk and held up my examination report. "You've done quite well on your test. You got a good score. It appears that you understand something about coding, Mr. Narvaez. Have you had any experience before?"

"Yes," I lied again. "At the university, I got a chance to work around the office."

"Good. Good." For a moment he stopped to concentrate on his pencil tip. "As you know, we're in urgent need of trainees. If you were hired, when could you start working?"

"Monday," I said quickly.

"Excellent. You're hired." We shook hands on the deal. As I got up to go, he stopped me. "Oh, one other thing. I'll need to see your high school diploma and your university transcripts."

"That's a bit of a problem, sir," I hesitated, not knowing what to say. "You see, everything I have is still back in Puerto Rico. It'll be coming over on the next boat, but it'll be some time before it gets here. Can you wait?"

"Sure. It's no rush. When you get them, just bring them in to show me. OK?"

I worked there for two years and they never did see any sign of those papers. The issue was soon forgotten.

For this job, I also had to be bonded. When I filled out the required papers, I once again had to lie, risking a perjury charge. I had to take my chances of being discovered, however, because I was desperate. Usually for bonding, the company checks your background thoroughly—but in my case, miraculously, they didn't. Today, I know this is just another example of how God watched over my affairs, and of his grace.

I worked as hard as I could at my new job. I was always on time and was always willing to work all the overtime they threw at me. I was a good worker—I had to be.

My superiors noticed my enthusiasm. At first, I started as a code clerk in the computer department, but soon graduated to a detail programmer. The stocks and bonds company was a good company to work for. When I put in an eight-and-a-half hour day, they paid me $2.25 for lunch, and when I worked nine hours, they paid me $5.00 for taxi fare. Every Monday, I would pick up an extra $20.00 to $30.00 in lunch and taxi-fare money. I proudly brought this bonus money home to Rosa.

At work, I wore a suit with a white shirt and tie. I had achieved my goal—I had my own desk with a name plate on it. I was happy. I felt I was finally coming up in the world. Still, I had a desire to improve myself further and obtain an even higher position. I wanted respect, authority and prestige; I wanted to be successful in the world's eyes. Therefore, on my own initiative, I started attending business school at night. I realized that while computer operators earned good wages, computer technicians earned even more. That became my goal.

Rosa and I had moved into the third-floor apartment of a tenement building in the Bronx. We settled down there into the comfortable routine of married life.

At first I found it difficult to be the instant father of three children. I knew that it would take time to gain their trust and I didn't try to force myself upon them. When I had been courting Rosa, I had met the children briefly on a number of occasions, but most of the time they had been asleep in bed. Now, we all needed time to adjust to one another, and to our new relationship.

They were cute kids: Rose Marie was almost six, the boy Tony was five, and the youngest, Eileen, was just out of her crib.

Rosie, as we called Rose Marie, had been deaf from birth. She couldn't express herself in the usual ways; she was often locked within herself and stubborn. My heart really went out to her. Slowly, I learned to speak to her in her own type of sign language. As the oldest, she took the longest time to accept me as her new father.

Tony and Eileen didn't really understand who I was—they just took my presence in the house for granted. Gradually, I won all of the children over. To express my love, I played with them, held them, kissed them, bought them lollipops, candy bars, and other little presents. I took them for walks to the park, the beaches, the zoo, the movies, and Coney Island. After several months had passed, the children finally started calling me "Daddy." It was one of the proudest moments of my life.

I really enjoyed having small children around. I had a lot of fun playing with them and romping in the snow. In the late afternoon, they would always play in front of our tenement building and watch for me to come home from work. When they saw me walking up the slope from the train station, they would run down that hill as fast as their little legs would carry them, racing each other to see who could reach me first. I would lift them high up in the air, and swing them around and hug them, and they would squeal in delight. To see them flying down that hill toward me, after a hard day of work, really made my day. Somehow, it made everything worthwhile.

Being a family man agreed with me. I enjoyed supporting a family, knowing that four people depended upon me. It gave me a sense of personal worth. For the first time in my life I felt I belonged somewhere, and that someone needed me.

I was promoted at work, and we began to do very well financially. Our bank account started to grow, and after all the bills were paid, we found that we still had something left over to spend at the movies and the pizza parlor.

Rosa and I were a relatively happy married couple. I was content with all the responsibilities of a married working man. I had no time to reflect about bitter memories of the past. My marriage and family were helping to heal me. During this time, I was more satisfied with my life than I had ever been before, yet something was missing. . . .

Sometimes Rosa and I would walk by the church on our block when they were having a street meeting and we would briefly stop to listen. Once or twice, I heard my old favorite song, "Washed in the Blood of the Lamb," being sung, and then a sharp pain would stab me. I would be reminded of other times and other places. It was as if the song were calling me—and I would hurry by, wanting to run.

The Lord had truly blessed me with a good job and a wonderful family. With his gifts of love, he was seeking to win me back.

TWENTY
Familiar Face

It was after eleven P.M. when we heard the knock at the door. Rosa and I were sitting in our living room, enjoying a quiet nightcap before retiring for the evening. The kids had been tucked into bed a long time ago and had been sound asleep for the last few hours. We looked at each other. We weren't expecting company. Who could it be?

I got up, motioning Rosa to stay where she was, and tiptoed down the hall to the door at the far end. It was dangerous in our area to open the door to anyone this late at night. Perhaps, I thought, it was someone in need of help, but even if it was, I still wouldn't be very anxious to open the door. There might be some kind of trouble and I didn't want to get involved. Usually, it was best to pretend that no one was at home.

Carefully I slid the covering off the peephole

and looked through the tiny magnifying glass. Outside the door a shadowy figure stood patiently waiting, his head bowed so that I couldn't see his face clearly. Something about the way he stood clicked in my mind.

"No, it couldn't be him," I thought to myself incredulously. I looked again, baffled. "It *is* him!"

Quickly I undid the four chains and safety locks and opened the door. My old friend Nicky Cruz stood there smiling at me. We hadn't seen each other in ten years. Dressed in a sharp suit and carrying a black attaché case, he looked very businesslike. My first impression of him was that he had joined the Mafia and become a professional hit man.

"Hey, c'mon in," I greeted him. "I haven't seen your ugly mug in years. What's been happening to you?" He walked in and we hugged each other. I was happy to see him.

"How you doing, man?" he asked, genuine concern in his voice.

"I'm OK. How you been?"

"OK."

"Well, don't just stand there. C'mon in," I urged him, closing the door and ushering him down the hall to the living room.

Nicky looked around. "You've got a nice apartment here," he remarked.

"Yeah. My wife's done a good job fixing the place up. Look, you want a drink? A beer or something?" It was a hot, humid night and I knew nothing would go down better than a cold beer.

He sat down in the arm chair and looked

directly at me, "No, thanks. I don't drink."

His answer surprised me. I had never known Nicky to turn down a drink before. Rather, I remembered him as a guy who drank like a fish, gulping down a whole bottle of wine and thinking nothing of it. Sometimes I thought he drank more "Thunderbird" than the company had put out! Something was very wrong here—his refusal to drink didn't make sense and I was suspicious. I couldn't figure it out, so I brushed the incident off as part of his professional training. Maybe he needed to keep himself calm and sober at all times if he was in the killing business.

Rosa came into the room just then, after checking up on the kids.

"Nicky, this is my wife Rosa," I introduced her and she smiled at our visitor. "Nicky and I used to hang around together a lot in the old days," I explained offhandedly.

"I'm married now, too." Nicky smiled. "I had to go all the way to California to meet Gloria, my wife. We're living out in Fresno."

Rosa sat down on the couch and listened to our conversation quietly, making herself inconspicuous. Nicky and I talked over old times and we shared a few laughs. Then the conversation took a sudden twist, when I asked him what I thought was a harmless question. "Hey, man, what you doing these days?" I asked him, eying his patent leather shoes and expensive suit. He had to be a man of the world to dress that way, I reasoned. "What you do? Join the Mafia or something?"

"No," Nicky laughed, but then he said very

soberly, his eyes never leaving my face, "I'm a minister."

I stared at him dumbfounded. "You! A minister? I don't believe it!" There was no way I could ever believe that this guy was a minister, not even in my wildest imagination. Not Nicky Cruz! I laughed at his joke.

"I'm serious, Israel. I'm a minister."

"I don't believe you, man. You're probably just pushing dope or something."

"No," Nicky said. "The only thing I'm pushing is the Lord Jesus Christ."

Something in his voice told me that he was sincere. He opened his attaché case and removed a large Bible. He held it up. "Look," he said, pointing to the inscription on the inside cover.

"Rev. Nicky Cruz," I read to myself, still not believing that it was possible. Slowly the truth of his words began to dawn on me. The last time I had heard of Nicky, he had been on his way to that preacher's home town in Pennsylvania. Surely, I thought, he would have grown tired of that religious nonsense long ago—but he hadn't. All the pieces fit together now: the way he was dressed, his mysterious behavior in refusing a drink. With the realization that he was indeed a minister, the real purpose for his visit, so unexpected and unannounced, suddenly occurred to me. I became angry.

"Well, I'll tell you something, man. If you came here to rap about God, forget it! You'd better split, man, because I don't want nothing to do with him or you!" I didn't want anybody, not even Nicky, to come to my home preaching to me, telling me what I did and did not have to do. I wouldn't put up with it. My affairs were my affairs.

"No, I didn't come here to talk to you about God, Israel," Nicky explained, trying to calm me down. "I know for some reason you're bitter."

Then he asked me gently, "Tell me what went wrong, Israel?"

A vivid picture of myself waiting on that street corner flashed across my mind, and with it a wave of bitterness. For a long time, I had been blocking this painful part of my past out of my mind. Deep down, I still harbored resentment against the attorney and the preacher for letting me down. I blamed God for the disappointment I had suffered. I wasn't sure now if I wanted to open up old wounds. . . .

"Yeah," I finally answered gruffly, "I'll tell you what went wrong. Remember that day when you and the attorney were supposed to pick me up and we were all going to drive out to Pennsylvania?"

Nicky nodded solemnly.

"Well, I waited on that corner for five hours and nobody showed up!"

"And then you went back to the gang?" Nicky asked quietly.

"Yeah, that's right," I said bitterly. "I thought all Christians were a bunch of phonies. . . ."

"Israel, I'm sorry—" Nicky shook his head sadly. "Somehow we missed you. I don't know how—we looked for you. Somebody had the street corners mixed up, I guess. . . ." He was lost in his own thoughts for a few minutes. "We always wondered what had happened to you. And then we heard that you had been arrested and sent to prison. We all felt bad—especially David. . . ."

"Yeah, well, forget it, man. There's nothing nobody can do about it now—" I tried to shake off the hostility that gripped me.

"Look, Israel," Nicky brightened, "I'm going to have a street meeting here in the city—in Manhattan. Why don't you come? There's going to be someone there I'd like you to meet. In fact, it's someone you already know."

I thought about that for a second. "There ain't gonna be anyone there I know unless it's someone from my family."

"No, she's not in your family," Nicky replied quickly. "But you're gonna know her when you see her."

"Well, I'll think about it," I told him, but I really wasn't interested in going to his meeting. All the same, he had intrigued me.

When Nicky left, Rosa asked me a few questions about our late-night visitor. I told her that he was one of the guys from the gang—but that didn't mean anything to her. She didn't know what a gang was. The gangs had disappeared from New York City a few years before. She wasn't surprised that a friend of mine had become a minister, either. She would have been, though, if she had known Nicky as I had known him. I didn't enlighten her. We turned off the lights and went to bed.

That night, I had a troubled sleep—Nicky's visit had disturbed me more than I cared to

240

admit. For a long time I lay in bed thinking about the way my life had gone since that day on the street corner when I had firmly turned my back on God. I thought about the gang, the night of the murder, and prison. . . .

"I wonder how my life would have turned out if I had gone with Nicky to Pennsylvania?" I pondered. "Where would I be now?"

The street corner meeting had been a turning point in our lives. Nicky had gone on from there to Bible College and become a minister. And I? I had gone onto prison and become a convict. Two lives—two separate journeys.

I had never really planned on going to Nicky's street meeting, but on the day that it was to be held, I somehow found myself on the subway train bound for Manhattan. Partly, I was going out of simple curiosity, for Nicky had aroused my interest in this mysterious girl and I wanted to see who she was, but that didn't fully explain my behavior. I found myself irresistibly drawn to the meeting, without really understanding why. My own actions surprised me; it was almost as if I was going against my will.

As soon as I got off the train, I could see a group of people gathered on the street in front of the station. The meeting was already in progress. The people had come to hear Nicky Cruz, known to them as one of the characters in the book *The Cross and the Switchblade*, and he was standing now on the makeshift platform, speaking to them.

Lounging against the station wall, a small

group of dirty, long-haired drug addicts idly listened to the man, for want of anything better to do. I stayed near them, in the shadow of the train station, listening to what was going on from a safe distance.

Nicky introduced the young lady that had joined him on the makeshift platform. She began to sing. As I listened to her voice, the way she sang touched me in some indefinable way. She put her whole heart into every word of the song, as if she really meant every word. I looked at her more closely. I didn't recognize her at first, but something about the way she was dressed and the way she sang stirred my memory. Then, just by coincidence or because Nicky had told her I might be there, she began to sing one of my favorite songs—the same song she had sung almost ten years ago at the St. Nicholas Arena youth rally, on the night I had accepted the Lord.

With a rush of memories, everything about that evening came back to me. Clearly in my mind, I could see her on the stage, trying to sing above all the hoots and catcalls that had greeted her valiant effort. In the end, the wild audience had been too much for her; she had burst into tears and fled from the stage. I had always thought she was very brave for what she attempted to do.

Why did I have to remember that night at the youth rally? Why couldn't I erase it from my memory? It didn't mean anything to me anymore—it was just another bad mistake, one of my many regrets.

When the young lady finished the song, Nicky came forward and preached. I was restless and wanted to leave right then—but something made me stay. Nicky's sermon was short. At the end, he invited those who wanted to accept Christ as their Savior to come forward. I was surprised to see a few of the drug addicts go and stand before the platform. Something in his message had reached them. Nicky prayed for them and then it was all over. The crowd began to disperse. Nicky looked in my direction and suddenly saw me for the first time. He called me over.

"Hey, man, I'm glad you made it. I want to introduce you to somebody." He put his arm around my shoulder and we walked over to the girl. She greeted us, all smiles.

"Israel, how are you doing? Are you still serving the Lord?" Her voice held genuine warmth, her eyes were bright and eager.

I frowned at her question. Bewildered, she looked from me to Nicky. Nicky quietly told her, "No, I'm afraid Israel isn't living for the Lord."

"That's right. Me and the Lord broke up many years ago," I said defiantly. Her question had made me angry. I didn't like anyone speaking to me about God.

She seemed startled, almost shocked for some reason. Maybe she found it hard to understand because she herself had always been so involved with the church. In dismay, she looked to Nicky for support and didn't say anything else after that.

Nicky turned to me, his eyes probing mine. "Could we pray?" he asked.

"It was my turn to be shocked. "Get out of here, man. I'll catch you later, OK? I just came to see who the person was that I knew. I'm glad I came; I'm glad I saw you again." I paused before I turned to go and then said grudgingly, "You're OK, man." I nodded to the girl, "It was nice seeing you."

I walked away from them both, knowing that their eyes were upon me, not knowing that they were praying for me, and disappeared inside the train station.

I did not know how many people across the country were praying for me. . . .

TWENTY-ONE
Reliving the Past

A few weeks later, Nicky came to see me again at my apartment.

"Listen, man, if you've come here to preach to me—" I stood at the door blocking the entrance. If he was planning to talk about God, I thought he might as well turn around and get out of my sight because I wasn't going to let him in and I wasn't going to listen.

Nicky laughed a short laugh. "Hey, man. Hold on. I haven't come to preach to you. I've come to ask a special favor of you." Suddenly he looked very serious. "It's got nothing to do with the church," he hastily assured me, "and it's very important to me."

"Yeah?" I said dubiously. I wondered if he was on the level.

He nodded his head. "Can we talk?"

"I guess so. Sure. C'mon in." I held the door wide open for him as he walked by me down the hall to the living room. I followed him. We sat down on opposite sides of the room—he on the sofa and I on a straight-backed chair. There was an awkward pause. I waited for him to speak. This time, I did not offer him a drink.

Nicky leaned back on the sofa and relaxed. "They're going to write my life story," he began and waited for my response. I didn't give him one. "It's gonna be called *Run Baby Run.*" He paused, thinking carefully about what he was about to say. "The writer would like to speak to you. You know more about the gang, Israel, than I do. You were there when it first started." His eyes met mine. "You can really help me. You're my friend. I believe that you are my friend."

"Well," I hesitated. "We're sort of friends."

"Can you help me out?" Nicky smiled charmingly. "Or should I say, will you help me?"

"Well," I answered slowly, turning the matter over in my mind. "I don't see no trouble in it. Sure, I'll help you."

His face broke into a broad grin. "I'll tell you what we're gonna do. I want you and your wife to come and have dinner with us at the Hilton Hotel. We'll have a good meal together and then we'll talk. How does that sound?"

"Pretty cool, man."

So a few evenings later, on October 31, 1967—I'll always remember the date—Rosa and I walked into the dining room at the Hilton Hotel all dressed up in our Sunday best. I hadn't told my wife what the evening was all about. She just thought that this was another night out on the town and that we were out for a good time. The maître d' escorted us to a large table near the back of the dining room. Nicky hailed us as we approached and introduced us to the two gentlemen sitting with him. One, a distinguished-looking man in his late forties, was Dan Malachuk of Logos International, the publisher of Nicky's book, and the other was Jamie Buckingham, the writer. I didn't think that he looked like a writer. Whenever I thought of writers, I pictured guys with long hair, beards, and berets—artist types. This man was clean cut and respectable looking.

As the evening progressed, I found that I was actually enjoying myself. The meal was excellent; the conversation lively. We were all relaxed and in a social mood and there was no tension among us. Nicky and I cracked inside jokes to each other about the old gang and he told me about some of the guys he had run into in recent years. Everyone laughed over our stories. I was having such a good time, I almost forgot that Nicky was a minister. He didn't try to preach to me once.

After we had finished our dessert and coffee, we all crowded into the elevator and went up to Nicky's suite on the eighth floor. When we were all comfortably seated, Nicky suggested that we begin with prayer, and everyone bowed his head. Everyone but me. I kept my eyes open. I didn't believe in prayer, but if they wanted to pray, it was OK with me. It didn't matter to me one way or the other.

Later, the writer switched on his tape recorder and started asking me question after question. The others listened politely as I told him all about gang life: the social activities, the initiation ceremonies, the rumbles, etc. We talked for many hours. Sometimes Nicky joined in adding his own personal observations and the producer asked some questions too. Rosa listened quietly to everything that I said—she was hearing most of it for the first time and I could tell that some of it shocked her. We had never talked about this part of my life before. Although she didn't interrupt me, her eyes never left my face.

The writer suddenly changed the subject. He popped a question at me—the last one that I would have expected.

"What happened to you that night at St. Nicholas Arena? At Rev. Wilkerson's youth rally?"

The question took me by surprise. "What on earth could that night have to do with Nicky's book?" I wondered silently. The question made me uncomfortable. All sorts of memories surfaced in my mind. Everyone was looking at me with intense interest, waiting for me to say something. The atmosphere in the hotel room seemed to change imperceptibly. It was heavy, close, charged. I didn't like it. I panicked.

"I don't want to talk about it," I said firmly. The subject was a little too religious for my liking. I glanced meaningfully at my watch. "Look, it's almost midnight. Rosa and I had better be heading home. It's late, we're tired, and I've got to be at work at seven in the morning. It's been a nice evening. . . ."

The writer interrupted my pat speech, "Israel, have you heard of *The Cross and the Switchblade*?"

"Nope. Never heard of it," I mumbled in

confusion. I wondered what he was getting at. "What about it?"

"Well, it's a book that was written by David Wilkerson and it sold over a million copies. You remember David Wilkerson, don't you?"

"I don't think that there's any way in the world that I could ever forget that dude," I frowned. It was an understatement.

"Well, your name is mentioned in this book that he wrote. . . ."

"Oh, it is, is it?" I was suddenly angry. What right had that preacher to use my name in his book? What had he said about me? Maybe I should sue him!

"If you want to help Nicky," the writer persisted, "if he's your friend, like you say he is, then you're going to have to tell us what happened that night at St. Nicholas Arena. It's important. A million people are out there praying for you and they want to know all about your experience."

I reconsidered his request. "Well, if it's gonna help Nicky's book—all right, I'll tell you. It's not gonna help me one way or the other. If it won't take long, I'll tell you."

"OK," he smiled eagerly. "Shoot."

So I started to tell them all about the unusual events of that Saturday evening almost ten years ago. Rev. David Wilkerson had arranged for a bus to pick us up and drive us to St. Nicholas Arena, the location of his youth rally.

"I had about fifty members of my gang, the MauMaus, waiting with me on a street corner. Nicky, you were there, remember? And you weren't too happy about going, either." I smiled at Nicky and he smiled back. "Anyway, we were listening to the latest groups on our radios—the Platters, the Flamingos, and the Penguins, which were all very popular with us. A few of the guys were crooning along: 'Shaboom. Shaboom' . . . . I was keeping an eye out for the bus which I thought would be a shiny new Greyhound. But the bus that finally pulled around the corner was nothing but a rickety-rackety, rusty old church bus, so 'gray' and old it couldn't 'hound' anymore. The bus driver—looking very religious in a bow tie and suit—opened the door for us and we all piled onto the bus, laughing and joking, drinking bottles of wine and smoking cigars. The bus driver's eyes bulged out. Some of us were only thirteen.

"I sat down on the right side of the bus and kept my eyes on the driver. I wondered what he was doing—his lips were moving real fast, like he was talking to himself. As we drove along, he hardly took his eyes off the rear-view mirror. I guess he was afraid that we were going to stab him in the back. When we got to the Arena, there were all kinds of enemy gangs gathered outside on the street watching us.

"'Man,' I said to Nicky, who was then my vice-president, 'there's gonna be a big rumble tonight. A lot of blood's gonna be spilled!' I turned to the rest of my boys. 'Keep cool. Just walk into the building now. If they don't start nothing, we don't start nothing.'

"Inside the door of the arena, an usher greeted us and asked who we were.

"'Man, don't you know? We're the MauMaus.'

"'Oh. Go to the right-hand section over there,' he indicated with a shaky sweep of his hand. 'That section's reserved for you and your gang.'

"So we jitter-bugged down the aisle, tapping our canes and looking around to make sure that our entrance had been noted. As we sat down, something weird happened," I told the writer, pausing for effect. "All the people in the first ten rows in front of us suddenly got up and scurried to the back like frightened rats! We looked over to the other side of the arena and saw another gang called the Bishops eying us. They were mostly Negro and they were from Brooklyn too. We were rival gangs and we were always fighting each other. We thought we were No. 1 and they thought they were No. 1. Now I knew that a rumble was going to break out for sure!

"Then a young lady came onto the platform. I could tell right away that she was religious: she had long hair, long sleeves, no makeup, and a long dress down to her ankles and up to her chin. She started to sing a gospel song.

"One of the Bishops jumped up. 'Right on, mama. You're comin' through!' He started to dance the Stroll down the aisle. Then some other dudes got up and started to grind and shake. Everybody was whistling and hooting and cat-calling.

"The young lady's voice cracked. She suddenly stopped singing and hurried off the platform, about to burst into tears. Then the preacher walked onto the platform and as he readjusted the microphone to his height, I noticed that you could hardly see his body behind the mike stand. I had to stop myself from bursting out laughing because he reminded me so much of the coyote who disappears behind a cactus in the 'Roadrunner' cartoon. I started to crack up.

"'Well, I am thankful that you have all come,' he greeted us. 'Before I begin my sermon tonight, we're going to do something different. We're going to collect an offering to help pay the expenses of renting this arena.' He held up six milk containers. 'Now I want some of you young people out there to come and help me take this offering.'

"Everybody raised their hands. Everybody wanted to 'take' the offering because that is exactly what they planned to do—take it and run. 'Hey pick me, man!' they tried to get the preacher's attention. 'Over here, preacher!'

"Nicky, my vice-president, and five of the other MauMaus were chosen for the honor. As they passed the milk containers down the rows, they would look at the change the people were dropping into them, then they would look at the way the people were dressed and shake their heads as if to say, 'Is that all you dudes think about your God? Are you that cheap?'

"I noticed that right from the first few rows, these boys weren't accepting any change tonight. Dollar bills, fives, and tens were jammed into the milk containers. Every now and then, they would push the money down with their fists to make room for more with a sinister grin on their faces.

"The boys went through the curtains to one

side of the platform. Everybody could read the 'Exit' sign blazing on the wall, pointing to the door behind the curtains. We all grew silent with suspense as we waited for them to appear on the platform. Some of the guys started to snicker. But then suddenly the six boys reappeared and walked across the platform over to the preacher. I knew something strange was going on. My boys looked confused and mixed up, as dazed as if they had just stepped out of a time machine.

"'Hey, man, what's happening?' I growled to myself.

"'Here, preacher,' Nicky cried angrily, thrusting his container into the preacher's hand. 'Here's your money and it's all there.' He was actually mad that he hadn't run off with it. It was against everything a MauMau stood for. The preacher grinned.

"As the boys made their way down the aisle to their seats, some of the other MauMaus started to 'boo' them. But all these guys had to do to silence the mockers was to give them a challenging look—they had a reputation that spoke for them. Then everybody calmed down."

Up until that point, I had been recounting all the events of that evening in an aloof, detached, matter-of-fact way. But now a strange thing happened: I really became involved in my story. I began to feel the same emotions I had experienced that night almost ten years ago. Everything came back. It was like reliving the past. My experience was suddenly vivid. Fresh. Alive. The words poured out of my mouth freely as memories flooded my mind, bursting through the dam

I had so carefully constructed against them. I forgot that I had an audience. It was as if I was talking only to myself.

"The preacher opened his Bible to begin his sermon," I continued. "As soon as he opened his mouth, I already knew his message. It was from John 3:16 and it was the same one that he had preached to us when we had first heard him on the street. 'For God so loved the world that he gave his only Son, that whosoever believeth in him should not perish but have everlasting life.'

"'Man, is that all that dude can talk about?' I groaned. 'That must be the only sentence he knows out of that whole Bible!'

"The preacher repeated the verse, stressing the 'whosoever believeth in him' part.

"'Whosoever believeth in him . . .' the preacher paused dramatically. 'That means that you Puerto Ricans have to love the Negroes. . . .'

"'No way, man!' I gritted my teeth. 'Not if they're Bishops.'

"'And you Negroes have to love the Italians,' the preacher continued. 'And you Italians have to love the Irish and you Irish have to love—'

"Suddenly, a white boy jumped up and cried indignantly, 'Man, you must be crazy! You say you want me to love those no-good niggers over there?' He ripped open his shirt to reveal a scar that stretched from his navel up to his throat. Somebody had gutted him wide open.

"Then a big Negro guy got up and yelled, 'Yeah, you filthy cracker! You're lucky we didn't cut your throat while we were at it!' That was the signal for a full-scale rumble. Everybody reached for their weapons and leaped to their feet. I clicked open my switchblade.

"'Shut up and sit down and listen to what I have to say!' somebody ordered. I looked around me, astonished. Nobody had the authority to order rival gangs around. Even a big shot from the police department would not have been able to calm us down at that moment. Yet, here was somebody ordering us all to sit down, somebody whose voice held authority and power. Turning around, I saw that it was that bag-of-bones preacher. He stood behind the microphone, pointing a bony finger out at the audience.

"'Now sit down and listen to me. This is the House of the Lord. I don't care what it was yesterday or the day before, today you're on holy ground and you're going to listen as you've never listened before. I know you think that blood is going to be shed all over the street tonight, but I'm going to tell you something. It's not going to be your blood. The blood of Jesus Christ is going to be poured upon your souls tonight. You're going to be made new creatures in him.'

"That caught me by surprise," I told the writer. "I sat down with the others.

"'Now, take those hats off your heads over there.' Strangely, we all obeyed. There was something about the authority in his voice. The auditorium became so quiet you could hear a cockroach scuttling across the floor.

"The preacher continued on with his sermon, presenting Jesus Christ in a way with which we could all identify—as the sharpest dude who had ever lived.

"'When he picked up that cross,' the preacher said, 'he was a man. He didn't need a gang. Oh, he had one. Up in heaven, he had the biggest gang the world had ever seen. At any time, he could have called down his gang and they would have slain all his enemies. . . .'

"'Man,' I thought to myself, 'I never knew Jesus was president of a gang. . . .'

"'Jesus,' the preacher continued, 'picked up his cross and bebopped all the way to Calvary, and he stumbled because he knew we were going to stumble someday, but he kept on going. And they crucified him. They took those spikes and they pushed them into his hands. They were man-made spikes. Not like your switchblades, that are so sharp they could cut through two leather jackets in a split second and cut a guy's gut wide open. No, they tore into his flesh and ripped it apart.'

"I thought about that. I turned my hands over, felt the soft flesh of my palms, and thought about those spikes being driven through Jesus' palms and feet.

"'You know something else?' the preacher asked. 'Jesus was a loner. Because on that day when he carried the cross, he was the loneliest man in the world. There was nobody by his side. His own followers, the members of his gang, had deserted him. Even his Father up in heaven couldn't look down upon him because he'd been made sin for us. . . .'

"Now I had had that happen to me. Sometimes when our gang had been rumbling, a few of the members had run out on us. Of course, they paid for it later. But I thought about what the preacher was saying. I thought of him hanging on that cross. All alone. I thought about how much he had suffered. Wow, this Jesus was some dude. It was really something for him to have done what he had done—in spite of everyone deserting him. He was a very lonely guy, in a ghetto by himself—just like me.

"'While you guys are so interested in gang-busting and cutting each other up, all you're doing is shoving your fist in his face,' the preacher continued. 'You're showing him that you don't care, just like people in those days didn't care. But you know, he cared so much for you, that he died for you. Even if you walk out of this building tonight and go to a gang fight, he still loves you. When he was dying on the cross, he called out to his Father, 'Father, forgive them for they know not what they do.'"

Suddenly the truth of those words again overwhelmed me. I couldn't go on with my story. I stopped talking. Before I knew it the tears were streaming down my cheeks.

"Jesus, what have I done?" I cried inwardly. For almost ten years I had been shaking my fist in his face. I had turned my back on him and hardened my heart to the gentle urging of the Holy Spirit. I had wallowed in bitterness, burned with anger, and choked on pride. In my rebellion, I had messed up my life. I had been involved in murder and I had wasted five years in prison. And all that time Jesus had still loved me! I realized that I had been running from him and now I wanted to stop running. The Holy

Spirit was moving in my heart and I was fighting him no longer.

"Jesus, forgive me," I sobbed. "Oh, forgive me!" All this time I thought *he* had let me down, but now I knew that it was *I* who had let *him* down.

I looked up at the others. Nicky was crying, the writer and publisher were crying. Even Rosa was crying. The Lord had touched her heart at the same time he had touched mine.

Nicky came over to us and asked if we would like to commit our lives to Jesus, to make a decision to live for him. Rosa looked at me. I quickly explained what was taking place. Then she nodded her head, her eyes brimming with tears. There in the hotel room, we bowed our heads and Nicky placed his hands on our heads and prayed over us. And then suddenly I was praying too, urgently at first and then, when I knew beyond a shadow of a doubt that he had forgiven me, more peacefully.

"Thank you, Jesus. Thank you." And then I was quiet, marveling in the inner knowledge of the change that had taken place—of the love that had replaced the hatred in my heart. And I knew, with certainty, the wonderful truth of St. Paul's words:

> . . . neither death, nor life, nor angels, nor principalities, nor powers, nor things present, nor things to come, nor height, nor depth, nor any other creature shall be able to separate us from the love of God, which is in Christ Jesus our Lord (Romans 8:38, 39).

Rosa and I got to our feet. We shook everyone's hand and then we left Nicky's suite. As we waited for the elevator, I put my arm around Rosa and she smiled up at me, radiant. There was a new bond of understanding between us. We had both experienced a new birth.

My ten long years of rebellion were over. Although my "journey back" to Christ had taken ten years, it had finally ended in victory—at the foot of the cross. The prodigal son had returned.

TWENTY-TWO
Flight to a
New Life

After Rosa and I accepted Christ as our Savior and Lord, our lives began to change slowly. One of the first things we did was to rid the apartment of things which we felt did not glorify Christ. We poured bottles of beer down the kitchen sink. We cleared out our liquor cabinet completely, draining many ounces of good whiskey. For awhile, the smell in our kitchen was overpowering. Our record collection dwindled by half as we tossed away all the records that we felt did not honor the Lord. We were sick of that kind of music, especially rock 'n roll, and had no desire to listen to it anymore. Surprisingly enough, the activities we had mainly indulged in, drinking and dancing, lost their attraction for us. Instead we had new interests. Almost every night after the kids were tucked into bed, Rosa and I pored over the Bible Nicky had given to us, eagerly devouring chapter after chapter. Of course there were many things we did not understand at first, but slowly our knowledge and insight grew.

Some people are under the mistaken impression that when one becomes a Christian, life suddenly comes up all roses. This is rarely the case, however, and it certainly wasn't in my experience! For the first few months after my conversion, everything in my life did appear to be going along unusually smoothly. I was lulled into a false sense of security. I was about to face an unexpected trial, however, a trial which I miserably failed. When the Enemy attacked, suddenly and without warning, he caught me completely unaware and unprepared, and almost succeeded in ensnaring me again. It happened this way:

I had already gone to work one morning, when Rosa, as usual, left the apartment with the children to walk the two oldest, Rosie and Tony, to school. We now had a baby girl, Susan, whom she carried, while little Eileen toddled along beside her. When she came back to the apartment, she discovered that the front door was open. At first she thought nothing of it, assuming only that Rosie, who had been the last one out that morning, had not shut it firmly. Unaware that anything was amiss, she had walked inside and down the hall before she spotted the shopping bags filled with loot outside one of the bedroom doors, ready to be carried away. She screamed. A young man ran out of the bedroom then, his pockets stuffed with anything he could grab at the last minute. He looked wildly around, saw

Rosa screaming and the two children crying, and ran straight toward them, knocking them down as he rushed out the door. None of the neighbors opened their doors to see what all the commotion was about. They probably thought it was just another husband and wife spat, or if they did suspect it was some sort of trouble, they didn't want to get involved. Badly shaken, Rosa phoned me at work, sobbing out the story.

I rushed home immediately. My first thought was for the safety of my family. I was relieved to find that, except for a bad case of fright and a few bruises, they were unharmed. When Rosa had been knocked down, she had managed to hold the baby in such a way that the child's head had not struck the floor. I thanked God for this.

It wasn't too difficult to discover how the burglar had made his entry. The kitchen window was wide open. I frowned. Usually the safety latch kept it tightly shut, but for some reason this morning it had been left undone. I bolted it properly. Ruefully I looked down into the alley below. A circular fire escape, hugging the building, passed near enough to this window to make it a simple matter for an agile thief to swing from the landing to our window and crawl through. It wasn't the first time it had happened. Once we had gone to the beach one Saturday, only to return and find that our television set had been stolen. Living in the area we lived in, I almost expected break-ins.

I checked the apartment to see what had been taken. The shopping bags stuffed with our belongings were still in the hallway where the thief, in his haste to depart, had left them. Our portable TV set was on the floor beside them, unplugged and ready to be hauled off. The jewelry that Dan Malachuk had given to us as a present, and other valuables that we had kept in our bedroom, were missing.

Though the cash value of these stolen goods did not amount to a great loss, the act of the burglary itself incensed me. I was furious. Someone had invaded my private property and could have killed my wife and children. The old primitive urge to kill swept over me, just as it had in my youth when a rival gang had invaded my turf. "When one of my family gets hurt, it's time to kill. . . ." Rage, not common sense, took control of my actions. I never even thought about trusting God in this situation. I never stopped to pray.

The next thing I knew, I was looking for a gun. From the description Rosa had given me of the burglar, I knew he had to be a dope addict, and dope addicts could be dangerous. In their anxiety to get a fix, they stopped at nothing. We didn't have a gun in our apartment, so I went to my brother's place. He didn't have one either. Undaunted, I visited David, the dope addict I had known in prison, who lived only a few blocks away. He was familiar with all the addicts in the area, and from my description, he was able to narrow the suspect down to a few possibilities. I offered him ten dollars to track our burglar down. He needed the money badly. Ten dollars could buy him two shots of heroin, and he would sell off his mother for less.

A few days later, David contacted me. He told me the dope addict-burglar's usual hangout. Since the place he mentioned wasn't too far from where I lived, I decided to take a little stroll through that neighborhood. I wasn't sure what I would do to him if and when I found him, but I certainly was going to mess him up good, if not kill him.

In the next few hours, I scouted the streets but found no one who fit the burglar's description. Finally, I stopped at the corner grocery store and told the owner who I was looking for. He nodded his head at my description. He knew him all right.

"But, hey, you better not mess around with that guy," the owner warned me. "He's real mean."

I drew myself up to my full height, unable to ignore the challenge. "Yeah, well, I just finished doing time in prison for killing someone and I'll kill again if I have to. Get it? If you see this punk, give him that message."

The owner blanched. "Oh. OK. . . ."

I stalked out of the grocery store and went home.

Praise the Lord that I never did find that guy! If I had, I might have lost my temper, and ended up in the joint again, serving out a life sentence for murder. The Lord, in his wisdom, allowed the burglary to take place, and used it for his purpose, as we were about to find out.

A week later we got a telephone call from Nicky Cruz in California. It was three A.M. New York time, but that didn't stop Nicky. In his excitement to talk to us, he must have forgotten the time difference between the east and west coasts.

"Israel!" his voice bubbled over the telephone. "I've got some wonderful news for you, brother!"

"Yeah . . ." I said sleepily, thinking that it had better be good to disturb me at this hour. "What kind of news?"

"Well, my church has decided to donate all the money needed to fly you and your family out to California! You can come and live here and help me with my new center, Outreach for Youth, that I'm opening in Fresno and . . ." breathlessly he spilled out all his plans.

I interrupted him, "Nicky. I'm not going, man."

"But why?" He seemed puzzled.

"Because I've got myself a good job with a good future. I'm on my way to becoming a computer operator. I'm going to be making some big money pretty soon."

"Well," Nicky wasn't at all discouraged, "you just pray about it and whatever the Lord puts upon your heart, you do it. OK?"

I agreed and hung up. The next morning over breakfast, I told Rosa about the telephone call and Nicky's plans. We didn't have much time to discuss the matter, because I had slept in and was in a hurry to get to work. I was just about to fly out the door when someone knocked on it. Who could that be so early in the morning?

I opened the door and was surprised to find a woman in her late forties smiling at me. I had never seen her before.

"Hello," she said. "I've just come from Puerto Rico. You don't know me, but somebody told me you were moving and I'm looking for an apartment."

I stared at her, baffled. We had told no one that we were moving. Until three o'clock this morning, we had never even thought about it! Who could have told her? I knew one thing, she couldn't have been standing outside the door at 3 A.M. listening to our telephone conversation. I looked at my wife and she looked at me. We were both mystified. Then it seemed to strike both of us at once. Perhaps Somebody was telling us to move out of New York and move out quickly! Could God have sent this lady to show us his will?

"Well, we may be moving out," I told the woman. "I don't know for sure. We may be moving to California."

"Oh, praise the Lord!" she clasped her hands. I knew apartments were hard to find in New York City, especially an apartment in a fairly decent building, but I thought she was getting a little over-enthused about it. She was positively beaming. "I just knew that this was the place I had to come to! Look, I don't have much money. Just a couple of hundred dollars. But I'll be glad to buy the apartment from you and anything else in it you won't be taking with you."

"Well, we're gonna leave half this furniture." I began. "And we won't be needing pots and pans and things like that. . . ."

"Oh, praise the Lord!" she burst out again. I was a little surprised by her joyful exclamations at the time, but now I realize that she was just thanking the Lord for what he was providing, and she was also glad that she had obeyed his voice in coming to our apartment.

That night Rosa and I discussed the idea of moving to California. I knew that if I went I would be giving up a good secure job and a possible promotion in the near future. I would be throwing away all I had worked so hard to obtain. Still, if the Lord wanted me in California to help Nicky Cruz with his youth center, then I would be much better off doing what he wanted me to do. I had real struggle in my heart over this decision. I sought the Lord in prayer.

Rosa liked the idea of moving, pointing out that our neighborhood wasn't a safe place to raise kids. The burglary was brought to my mind again, and I shuddered. Perhaps the Lord had allowed that to happen so that it would be an extra incentive for us to move. Once David Wilkerson had tried to get me out of New York, but I had never made it. Now Nicky was trying. The Lord didn't seem to want me to hang around this area anymore. He wanted me out of the state in a hurry. This time he wasn't taking any more chances of me falling back into my old way of life.

We made up our minds. We were going to step out in faith and trust the Lord for our future. We were leaving.

As the plane took off, I reached for Rosa's hand and uttered a prayer. The baby, Susan, was sleeping peacefully on her lap. The other kids,

Rose Marie, Tony, and Eileen had their faces pressed to the window pane. We were all excited. This was going to be my first airplane trip.

Air-borne, I gazed out of the window at the city of New York sprawled out below me. From this perspective, even the skyscrapers seemed dwarfed and insignificant. All of my life, I had been trapped in the dead-end alleys and endless streets of the concrete jungle below. . . .

Now as the plane climbed higher, we broke through the clouds and I was dazzled by a clear blue sky. I felt a tremendous burst of freedom within me. At last I would be leaving New York behind. Memories of the ghetto, the gangs, the murder, the wasted years in prison, the struggle to make it in society—all these shackles that had once bound me fell away. I was free! I was reborn in Christ and I was beginning a new life in California, serving him. I was beginning a journey that would not end until I met Jesus. Right now, floating over the clouds, that day didn't seem to be so very far away.

I squeezed Rosa's hand and she smiled at me. We didn't know what the future held for us, but we were content to know who held the future!

TWENTY-THREE
Channeled into Ministry

When the plane touched down in Los Angeles, it was dark outside. We would have to wait until morning to see what our newly adopted state of California looked like. Rosa carried Susan and I had Eileen slung over my shoulders like a sack of potatoes as we crossed the runway into the airport teminal buildings. We were all tired from the flight but excited to be on the threshold of a new life.

Nicky was there at the airport to welcome us. We hugged each other. He collected our suitcases and then we all piled into his car. In no time the kids were asleep in the back seat, but I was wide awake as we drove for three hours to the city of Fresno. Finally Nicky pulled the car up in front of a large modern house on a tree-lined street in a quiet suburban neighborhood. Rosa nudged my arm in excitement as we followed Nicky up the path to the front door. He unlocked it and stepped to one side for us to enter.

Inside, we could hardly believe our eyes! I had been expecting to find a cold, empty house but I was in for a pleasant surprise. A little Christmas tree had been set up near the fireplace and underneath it were many greeting cards wishing us the best in our new home. Also spread around the base of the tree were all sorts of gifts and useful kitchen utensils we would need to set up housekeeping. Some of the envelopes contained cash—a total of $450.

The kids ran in and out of the bedrooms and Rosa and I followed more slowly, stunned. We wandered through our new home, open mouthed and flabbergasted. Much of the furniture we thought we would have to buy had already been provided for us—beds, chests, chairs, tables—even a living room sofa. Crates and cardboard boxes stacked high in the hallway promised more. In the kitchen, Rosa opened the cupboards and stood back, amazed to find each shelf stocked with cans of food. I opened the freezer and found a whole half side of beef. Rosa stared at me, absolutely astonished, her eyes brimming with tears. She pulled out a chair and sat down on it and soon she was weeping unabashedly. I went over and hugged her tenderly.

"I—I didn't know," her voice broke, "that there were still such kind people left in the world. . . ."

But there were. God's people. Nicky told us later that a lot of people from different churches had gotten together to prepare this house to receive its new family. Truly, these kind souls had entered into the spirit of Christmas. As I looked around at all they had done in love, I thanked God for his marvelous provision and for his wonderful people.

Later I found out that our house had been the object of some considerable interest for the past few weeks. It had been a hub of activity. Neighbors had watched in curiosity, as every day new groups of people arrived, carting chairs and lamps and tables and crates and boxes. Others came with brooms and mops and paint brushes. They couldn't understand what was going on, but they had witnessed true Christian sharing.

The next morning, our first morning in California, we were all up bright and early. We stepped out into the backyard to see what California looked like in the daylight. It was warm and sunny outside—yet Christmas was only a few days away. Back in New York, it was dirty and sooty and slushy at this time of year, but that all seemed very far away.

The kids ran around on the grass, whooping in delight. On each side of the yard, two large orange trees grew, their boughs overladen with fruit, touching the ground. The kids, like a swarm of locusts, attacked first one and then the other tree, stuffing their mouths with fresh oranges. They didn't care that the oranges were not ripe yet and not ready for picking. Later they would be sorry, but for the moment they gorged themselves.

When they finished with the orange trees, they occupied themselves with the grapes which grew in thick clusters along the back of the redwood fence that enclosed the yard. I'm sure they thought that the good Lord had placed them right in the middle of the Garden of Eden.

The following Sunday we went with Nicky and his wife Gloria to their church. It was an Assembly of God church that boasted a large congregation, but now during the Christmas holidays it was packed to overflowing. More than eight hundred people were jammed into the building and we had trouble finding seats. When the usher finally cleared us a section, the pastor was already opening the morning worship service and greeting the congregation from behind the pulpit. He stopped in the middle of what he was saying as he saw our group being seated.

"Oh, I see that our guest from New York City has just arrived! How many of you have read the book *The Cross and the Switchblade*?" An excited murmur swept through the crowd and almost all those present raised their hands. The pastor beamed. "Good. I'm glad so many of you have read that book, because this morning we have an evangelist with us here who is one of the main characters in that book. Many of you know him."

I glanced at Nicky, thinking that the pastor was referring to him. He was the only evangelist I knew that was there from that book. Nicky kept his eyes steadily on the pastor.

"Brother Israel," the pastor's voice boomed out over the microphone, "will you please come to the pulpit, my brother, and just share with us what the Lord has done in your life."

I sat stunned, not believing what I was hearing. I turned to Nicky. "You lousy no-good rat,"

I growled in his ear. How could he, my friend do this to me? I wasn't going up to the front, not in front of all those people! No way!

"Israel," Nicky whispered to me, "he's calling *you*. These are the people who paid your way out here. They love you. You're not going to hurt their feelings by not going up there, are you?"

"There's no way, man. I'm not going." I was adamant.

"Come, my brother. Please," the pastor urged me. "Come up to the platform here."

I wished I could sink into the bench. It seemed everybody had turned around in their pew and was staring at me. It was no use stalling any longer. I could see that the pastor was going to hold up the whole service to wait for me to come forward.

I stood up and made my way slowly down the aisle. I felt like every eye in that entire church was glued upon me. I kept my eyes on the floor. Some grandma reached out as I was passing her and grabbed me by the arm.

"God bless you, son."

I mumbled something in reply and kept on going. At last I climbed the steps to the platform. The pastor came over from behind the pulpit to meet me halfway. He reached out his arms and clasped mine, then gave me a bearhug. After so many years in prison, my automatic reaction was to push him away. I backed away slightly. He didn't take any notice.

"Praise the Lord, brother!" he said exuberantly. "It's good to see you. Now, share with us what the Lord has been doing in your life all these years in New York City. And tell us about your wonderful ministry in the ghettos!"

Evangelist! Ministry! Boy, did he have the wrong person! I didn't know what to say. I stood up there behind that pulpit and looked out at the sea of faces that were waiting expectantly for me to speak. If they were thinking that another Billy Graham had come into their midst, they were mistaken! I found my voice at last.

"Well, thank you. I just want to thank all of you for the wonderful home and the food and everything. I, uh, I . . ." I was stuck for words. The only thing that came into my mind was John 3:16, so I repeated it, "For God so loved the world that he gave his only begotten Son, that whosoever . . ." I rattled it off so fast that all the words slurred together and became unintelligible. I finished breathlessly, "God bless you." And I ran off the platform and down the aisle to my seat.

There was a pregnant pause. The congregation wasn't sure what had just taken place. If they had been expecting some great words of spiritual encouragement, I'm afraid they were disappointed.

The people sitting behind me tapped me on the shoulder. "God bless you. It's nice to meet you," they whispered, and I felt better.

As soon as the service was over, I was out of my seat and into the car in about five seconds flat. I didn't want to ever go through that again.

The Lord, however, had other plans. On Monday morning the telephone began to ring. The pastor of another church in Fresno was on the line. "Praise the Lord, brother," he said. "We heard that you were in town and that you were going to live among us. Can you come to our church this Sunday for the evening service and share with us what the Lord has been doing in your life?"

"Well, uh, uh, I dunno . . ." I said lamely, trying to think of some excuse.

"Good. Then you can come. Praise God," the pastor said before I could contradict him. "I'll mark the date down on my calendar. You write it down on yours too. We'll see you then."

That was the first phone call of many. Word that I was now living in Fresno spread rapidly. Pastors from all denominations were asking me to speak in their churches: Baptists, Pentecostals, Lutherans, Presbyterians, Alliance. I didn't believe in waving any flag except that of Jesus Christ, so I went to all of them, speaking wherever I was wanted.

Before I knew it, I was traveling to Los Angeles and San Francisco, and then even farther abroad to cities out of the state and, finally, all over North America. I hadn't even heard of most of the places, let alone known where they were. I just went where the Lord sent me: My ministry opened up as simply as that. The Lord began to use me. For the next two years, I had speaking engagements lined up for almost every weekend.

The center for Outreach for Youth that Nicky was starting in Fresno had trouble finding a building from which to begin its operation. Many of the kids that came to Nicky for help ended up staying at our home for awhile. I had a chance to talk with them. Most of them were just mixed-up kids. During this period, we lived on our savings, but that soon dwindled away, and Nicky often had to come to our rescue by paying our rent. It became obvious that I needed to get a job and so, when a Christian brother from our church offered me one, I gratefully accepted. When Nicky's center finally found a building, and a position with his organization became available shortly after, I was passed over in favor of a Bible school graduate who, the board thought, was better qualified. At this time I briefly considered going to Bible school myself, but in the end I didn't feel that the Lord was calling me in that direction. Certainly with a wife and now five kids to support, it would have been difficult for me to have gone anyway. The Lord had brought me to California, but it was not his will for me to become a part of Nicky's Outreach for Youth program.

Instead, he was leading me in a different direction. One of the first speaking engagements I had was inside a juvenile detention home. When they had first asked me to give my testimony there, I was reluctant. Five years had passed since I was behind bars, but prison still held horrible memories for me. I had promised myself that I was never going to go behind those walls again and now they were asking me to do just that. I knew, though, that the Lord wanted me to go there. He wanted me to face the past. But not alone. He would be with me. It would be part of the healing process he had in store for me.

On the appointed day, a Christian brother

came to my house to pick me up. As we drove along, Brother Huenergardt confided in me, "I've been a Christian for a long time now, Israel. I haven't lived your kind of life. When I speak to those boys at the home, it seems to count for nothing. They don't listen to me because I haven't gone through what they have. I haven't experienced their kind of life first hand. You have. They'll listen to you."

I wasn't so sure. I had no idea how they would react to what I had to say to them. I had my misgivings.

A guard led us down the long corridors of the detention home, unlocking doors in front of us, and after we had passed through, relocking them again behind us. As each one of those steel doors was opened, forgotten doors of my memory also swung open. The fears of five long years leaped to life again. I felt like an inmate again, doomed to walk down these dark corridors forever. I could almost hear the audible voice of a guard yelling at me, "Get in there, No. 12, get a move on," and then the click of the cell door locking into place, leaving me suddenly alone in a cell. In my mind, that "click" of a prison door had replaced the "click" of a switchblade opening for its ability to induce in me a dull terror. I looked over my shoulder and saw the guard locking the last door behind me and I thought, "Oh, man, get me out of here." But there was to be no escape for me now.

The guard led us into one of the classrooms used for teaching lessons. A young man was seated at the front, strumming his guitar and singing gospel songs with a country and western flavor. The boys were already beginning to shuffle into the classroom. They were mostly eleven-, twelve- and thirteen-year-olds, and they looked pathetically young to be locked up in a place like this. My heart went out to them. I studied their faces and picked out the bold ones, the mean ones, the shy ones. And in some of their faces, I could see myself.

I was surprised to see how many boys were filing into the room. Word had spread along the prison grapevine that an ex-gang leader from the streets of New York City who had himself done time was going to speak to them. They looked at me sullenly, their faces hard and closed.

Brother Huenergardt introduced me and I began to give them my testimony. It was very crude, and filled with lots of slang words.

"Hey, you guys are nothing but a bunch of suckers. You think you're so cool, you're so slick. Maybe you're pushing dope and you're popping pills and you think you're pulling the wool over everyone's eyes, but you're only pulling it over your own. You're building a real cool front for yourselves. But hey, look where you are. You think you are so smart, but every one of you got caught. And so here you are now, behind bars. What a bunch of chumps!"

My words had struck home, but some of them didn't like it. They were bristling with anger. A few looked like they were about to get up and leave. My next words stopped them.

"The reason I can talk to you in this way," I told them, "is that I've been a sucker just like you've been, and it cost me five years of my life."

That was the breakthrough. I had their full attention. I launched into the story of my gang life and the murder, and then I told them about my experiences in prison. The Spirit of the Lord was moving among them. The boys had stopped their restless squirming. They were all ears. It was really wonderful how the Lord was using these incidents from my life to reach them.

"You're only in kindergarten now," I told them. "Some of you will go on to high school . . . the reformatory. And if you get your diploma there, you'll graduate to college, the state prison, and from that moment on your life will repeat a never-ending cycle. Prison will be a revolving door for you." I paused to let the full effect of my words sink in. "But it doesn't have to be like that. Jesus Christ is the door of life. If you go through him just one time, you can have eternal life forever."

I stopped talking. The room was silent. No one moved. Brother Huenergardt, who was very receptive to the ways of the Lord, came and stood beside me. He put his arm around my shoulders and said very softly:

"You've heard his story, haven't you? If Jesus changed this man's life, Jesus can change your life too. I wonder how many of you out there right now are thinking about what's happened to this man's life? Are you walking the same road that this man was walking . . . the road that leads to prison and death? You know, you don't have to walk that road. There's another one—a road that leads to freedom and life. Which road are you going to take? The decision is yours. Right now, Jesus can change your life. Right now, right this very moment. Just raise your hand, right where you're sitting, right now, any one of you who would like to accept Jesus Christ. . . ."

One by one the boys began to raise their hands. Some of them were sobbing quietly. I knew that the Spirit of the Lord was really breaking their pride, because you don't cry in prison. It's a sign of weakness. I counted their raised hands. There were over sixteen.

"Wow!" I thought to myself, humbled. "I didn't think that the Lord could use my testimony like that." But he had. I knew it wasn't only my words that had reached those boys, but the power and presence of the Holy Spirit moving in their hearts, convicting them of their sin and the truth of my words. Praise the Lord! I realized right then that a testimony, even one as crude as mine had been, was a powerful tool in the hands of the Lord.

Brother Huenergardt asked the boys who had raised their hands to come forward. The others were dismissed. We prayed with them and talked with them and gave them tracts of the book of John. Brother Huenergardt took down their names for follow-up purposes. We left the juvenile home that day very tired, but very happy.

EPILOGUE

It is hard to believe that it is more than a decade since the night I recommitted my life to Christ.

These past years have not been uneventful. They have been filled with much joy and sorrow, victory and tragedy.

The first time that I returned to New York City, it was to attend the funeral of my oldest sister, Aurelia. She had mixed sleeping pills with alcohol and died in her sleep. Nobody knows whether it was an accident or not. At the funeral parlor, her oldest son took his high school ring and slipped it onto her finger. A few hours later it had disappeared—somebody had stolen it.

At the graveside, my mother asked me to say a few words. I had a chance to witness to my family and relatives about the love of Jesus Christ.

Less than a year later, I returned to the east coast once again—this time, for the funeral of my oldest brother Benjamin. He had been hit and instantly killed by a train—a tragic death. My mother was really crushed to have two of her nine children die in such a short time and at such a young age—both were only in their thirties. The deaths brought our family closer.

The death of loved ones is always hard to bear, but it is especially hard when they are unsaved. It grieved me to think that my brother and sister died without knowing Jesus as their Savior. I wondered if I could have reached them for Christ if I had had more time. Sometimes it seems that the hardest people to witness to are the members of your own family. The only comfort I have is that perhaps in those last seconds before death, my brother and sister might have cried out, "Oh, my God, forgive me, help me. . . ." Nobody knows.

During this period of mourning, the Lord gave me one reason to rejoice. I discovered that my brother Albert had accepted Jesus. I was so happy because now there was another member of my family who had come to know the reality of Christ. The Lord had answered my prayers. Albert's conversion was like a promise of others to come.

Our oldest daughter, Rose Marie, now seventeen, has been deaf from birth. After I had attended one of Kathryn Kuhlman's meetings, and witnessed many miracles, I thought that if I brought my daughter to a meeting, the Lord would heal her. I hoped the Lord would use Kathryn, his servant, to open Rose Marie's ears. Of course, the Lord doesn't work according to our plans. His ways are not our ways. Rose Marie was not healed.

Not long after that, however, our daughter Eileen's skin color began to change and she got very sick. The doctor informed us that she had a kidney infection and if her condition didn't improve, she would have to have one of her kidneys removed. I prayed that this would not have to happen, but that the Lord would touch and heal her.

I believe the Lord answered my prayers, because shortly after, Kathryn Kuhlman held a meeting in Fresno. The auditorium was jampacked and many healings took place. After the meeting was over, I took my daughter to the back rooms. At first Kathryn's manager wouldn't let us in to see her—she was exhausted—but then Kathryn herself called us in.

"Oh, Israel, how are you?" she asked. She knew me because she had interviewed me on her TV program.

Then she walked straight over to Eileen. "The Lord's just asked me to pray for you. Come over here." She prayed for Eileen and then said, "The Lord's going to do something wonderful in your life."

When we next took Eileen to the doctor, she was perfectly OK. And she's still healthy and beautiful today, for which we praise God.

Today, I am a minister of the gospel, living in Seattle, Washington. I give my testimony in churches, auditoriums, schools, and prisons, and on radio and TV programs all across North

America. Wherever I have spoken, young boys and girls have come up to me and said, "Boy, if I had a testimony like yours, the Lord could sure use me!" I explained to them that the Lord could use anybody. I believe that young people who are so often overlooked can be greatly used for the Lord. My recently formed association, "Association for Youth Evangelism," has purposed to train young people in witnessing for the Lord.

Sometimes when I look back on those ten lost years—wasted years in which I rebelled against God, I am tempted to think:

What if the attorney had picked me up? What if I had gone to Pennsylvania to see Rev. Wilkerson?

What if I hadn't turned my back on God and gone to prison?

How would my life be different now? Where would I be in the ministry today?

To this day, I do not know how the street corner mixup occurred. While I had been waiting on my corner, Myrtle and Flatbush, the attorney who was supposed to pick me up had driven by another corner, Myrtle and DeKalb. Who was responsible for this misunderstanding? Nobody knows for sure. But how or why this error occurred is not really important. What is important, however, is my own reaction to it. Although we cannot always choose the circumstances or events that happen to us, we *can* choose our own attitude toward those circumstances or events. In my case, I chose to be angry. I allowed a root of bitterness to grow within me, allowed my heart to harden to the Holy Spirit. I turned my back on God and closed my ears to his voice. Because I wasn't solidly grounded in God's Word and did not have knowledge of his ways, I stumbled. That's why it's so important for Christians, especially new Christians, to study the Bible, so that in time of temptation or adversity, they can remain steadfast.

> For we wrestle not against flesh and blood, but against principalities, against powers, against the rulers of the darkness of this world, against spiritual wickedness in high places. Wherefore take unto you the whole armour of God, that ye may be able to withstand in the evil day, and having done all, to stand (Ephesians 6:12, 13).

Of course I realize it is futile to wonder how my life would be different if I hadn't rebelled against God. I know that the Lord can use everything that has happened to me for his glory—he has a purpose and plan for my life. In his wisdom, the Lord allowed the street corner mixup to occur. He allowed me to go to prison, where he was by my side every step of the way—though I stubbornly refused to acknowledge his presence. He had his hand on my life. Even though I had turned my back in defiance against God, he remained faithful to me.

Although my prison sentence was not part of God's perfect will for my life, I believe that it may have been his plan to keep me from drugs, the gangs, and an early grave—to save me from myself. He took me out of society and placed me in an environment where I was forced to follow the law.

God did not send me to prison, however—I sent myself. Prison was the end result of my own disobedience and rebellion. As the Bible says:

> Thine own wickedness shall correct thee, and thy backsliding shall reprove thee: know therefore and see that it is an evil thing and bitter, that thou hast forsaken the Lord thy God, and that my fear is not in thee, said the Lord God of hosts (Jeremiah 2:19).

Today, instead of looking back and regretting what may have been, instead of tormenting myself with what I could have done for the Lord in those ten wasted years of backsliding, I am looking to the future, and taking full advantage of my second chance. As St. Paul says:

> Wherefore seeing we also are compassed about with so great a cloud of witnesses, let us lay aside every weight, and the sin which doth so easily beset us, and let us run with patience the race that is set before us (Hebrews 12:1).

And that's what I'm doing. I'm in Jesus' gang now and I'm fighting for souls. I'm running the race to obtain that crown.

Readers may contact me
at the following address:

Israel Narvaez
Association of Youth Evangelism
P. O. Box 5328
Seattle, WA 98105